Jacobo Schifter, PhD

From Toads to Queens
Transvestism
in a Latin American Setting

"**I** have read with great pleasure Jacobo Schifter's *From
Toads to Queens.* Using his sharp
observation skills as a social researcher, Dr. Schifter has conducted a thorough investigation
of a thus-far neglected population. Combining quantitative and
qualitative methods, the author
offers both broad and in-depth
perspectives on his subject matter.
Dr. Schifter succeeds in present-
ing a vivid and compelling picture
of the hard lives of transvestites in
Latin America."

Alex Carballo-Diéguez, PhD
Research Scientist,
HIV Center for Clinical
and Behavioral Studies,
New York State Psychiatric Institute
and Columbia University,
New York, NY

From Toads to Queens
Transvestism
in a Latin American Setting

HAWORTH Gay & Lesbian Studies
John P. De Cecco, PhD
Editor in Chief

From Toads to Queens
Transvestism
in a Latin American Setting

Jacobo Schifter, PhD

Harrington Park Press
An Imprint of The Haworth Press, Inc.
New York • London • Oxford

Published by

Harrington Park Press, an imprint of The Haworth Press, Inc., 10 Alice Street, Binghamton, NY 13904-1580

Cover design by Jennifer M. Gaska.

The Library of Congress has cataloged the hardcover edition as:

Schifter, Jacobo.
    [De ranas a princesas. English]
    From toads to queens : transvestism in a Latin American setting / Jacobo Schifter.
        p.   cm.
    ISBN 0-7890-0649-9 (alk. paper)
    1. Transvestism—Costa Rica—San José. I. Title.
HQ77.2.C8S3513 1999
306.77—DC21
                                                                            98-46116
                                                                                  CIP

ISBN: 1-56023-958-1 (pbk.)

CONTENTS

ABOUT THE AUTHOR

Jacobo Schifter, PhD, is the Regional Director of ILPES (the Latin American Health and Prevention Institute), an AIDS prevention program financed by the Netherlands' government. One of the most prolific writers in Latin America, Dr. Schifter wrote books on the Costa Rican civil war, U.S.-Costa Rican relations, and Costa Rican anti-Semitism before shifting his interests when AIDS started to affect the Central American region. He then established the first regional institute to fight the epidemic and created dozens of innovative programs, such as AIDS hotlines and AIDS prevention workshops for Latin gays, prisoners, street children, Indians, male sex workers, and other minority groups. He also started to publish controversial books on AIDS, including *The Formation of a Counterculture: AIDS and Homosexuality in Costa Rica* (1989), *Men Who Love Men* (1992), *Eyes That Do Not See: Psychiatry and Homophobia* (1997), and *Lila's House: Male Prostitution in Latin America* (1998). These books have become best-sellers in the region and have inspired many to join the fight against AIDS and homophobia as well as changed many Latin governments' discriminatory policies against people with AIDS.

Foreword

The title of this book neatly encapsulates its essence. *From Toads to Queens* draws both its magic and its challenging findings from the depth of intimacy and insight provided in the world of Latin transvestites. The tangible sense of this closeness is testimony to the willingness of those whose spirits are captured in this book to be so represented. In this sense, *From Toads to Queens* carries on the traditions of earlier feminist methodology that challenged the existing orthodoxy of objective dispassionate observation of one's research field, and insisted on the inclusion and acknowledgment of an empathetic relationship between researcher and researched. This is not only an intimate book, but one in which the vividness of language and description communicates the extent to which the author personally relates to his respondents.

The delight of this book is, as well, that it offers center stage to those who in many research projects are left with bit parts—the respondents themselves. Jacobo Schifter's contribution to the scholarship of sexuality goes further than his adventurous intellect, which illuminates corners of the existing landscape of sexual culture, while at the same time providing new lands for exploration. My pleasure in reading this book was enhanced by the clear agenda of the author to sit and listen, to allow the subjects themselves to speak—intellectual generosity that is as welcome as it is productive.

The importance of this book goes beyond that of the insights it offers into sexual identity and practice in a specific cultural context. If we are truly committed to a global interchange of ideas on sexuality and culture, we must acknowledge not just the distinctions but the similarities in these spheres. *From Toads to Queens* continues in the tradition established in *Lila's House* (1998) and evident in all of Jacobo's work—to ask questions of this subject that are, in effect, universally relevant, even as they are derived directly from and informed by the author's unique attachment to the multiple and diverse worlds of Latin sexuality. But *From Toads to Queens* builds and develops these characteristics, so much so that the task of proofreading was made more difficult by the distracting and infectious humor of the respondents, and of the equally vivid verbal pictures provided by their "amanuensis." This book is not only a pleasure to read, but does what all good intellectual works should do—it stimulates as many questions as it answers.

Gail Hawkes
Department of Sociology
Manchester Metropolitan University
England
Author, A Sociology of Sex and Sexuality
(Open University Press, 1996)

Preface

In 1989, ILPES (Latin American Institute for Health Education and Prevention), with financial assistance provided by the World Health Organization (WHO), carried out the first study ever undertaken in Central America pertaining to the incidence of HIV and AIDS among men who have sex with other men. Costa Rica was chosen as an appropriate research site, despite its small size, because of its visible and organized gay community, a community that is itself divided into many subcultures and subpopulations. Gay men were at the front line of the AIDS epidemic, making up approximately 75 percent of all reported AIDS cases. Finally, the country was thought to be representative of conditions elsewhere in Central America and the Caribbean basin.

The general aim of the research was to undertake a KAP (Knowledge, Attitudes, and Practices) survey for this community and identify risk factors leading to HIV infection among homosexual and bisexual men, as a basis upon which to develop appropriate education and prevention programs. Adopting a comparative approach, research was undertaken with various subpopulations of homosexual men, including transvestite sex-trade workers and gay bar patrons. In the present study, we make use of data from this earlier work where appropriate, for example in the preparation of the tables.

In broad terms, it is possible to divide the research program upon which this book is based into two distinct components. The first was quantitative in orientation, and involved the distribution of a structured questionnaire to a sample drawn from various groups of homosexual men. Of course, in this context it bears emphasizing that, given the impossibility of achieving a truly random sample of the country's transvestite population, generalizations cannot be made as to the incidence of the phenomena studied. By contrast, the second component was primarily qualitative in approach, consisting of in situ observation underpinned by in-depth interviews with key informants, the latter lasting for two to three hours.

The field work for the first part of the study was undertaken over the course of three months, from November 1989 to February 1990, with ten gay men hired to conduct the interviews. Having made contact with a prospective transvestite participant, interviewers proceeded to fill out each questionnaire in writing. Participants each received 1,000 colones (approximately U.S. $10 in 1990) in return for their involvement. Generally speaking, interviews were conducted in that part of San José where the majority of brothels were located (i.e., the central core and the city's southeastern zone), though in some cases interviews were also carried out in apartments, bars, or in the homes of transvestites who did not live in the brothel area. Moreover, given that some financial compensation was available to those who participated in the study, interviewees were generally willing to recommend other prospective participants to our staff. Through the use of this type of snowball sampling technique, a total of twenty-two transvestites completed questionnaires, with twenty of them also participating in an in-depth interview of approximately one hour in length. These interviews were conducted during the months of January and February 1990, with each participant being paid 1,000 colones per hour.

Once contact had been made with transvestites who were also sex-trade workers, it became feasible to interview their lovers as well, with eleven such interviews being carried out (again, 1,000 colones were paid to each participant). All but one of these interviews were tape recorded, with participants being assured of complete confidentiality and that none of the information gathered would be used against them. In accordance with participants' own wishes, only their professional names were used in the findings report.

A second study was launched by ILPES in 1997 to evaluate the degree of change over the course of the previous seven years, and to adapt education and prevention initiatives accordingly. Bearing this purpose in mind, a qualitative survey was undertaken, with twenty-five in-depth interviews being conducted with transvestite sex-trade workers, of whom the vast majority were based in San José's Clinica Biblica neighborhood. Interviews lasted anywhere from one hour to ninety minutes, and dealt with significant changes in participants' lives over the course of the past decade: relationships, money, drugs, jobs, love affairs, and problems with the police or the neighborhood.

This time individuals were paid 5,000 colones per interview (U.S. $20 in 1997), which was roughly equivalent to the hourly rate they charged their clients. Also, five in-depth interviews were carried out with sex-trade workers' lovers and, after the permission of the client in question was obtained, one sex session was audiotaped. Clients who agreed to participate in an interview were paid 5,000 colones, while 2,000 colones were paid to the individual who agreed to be taped during sex.

In order to gain a broader understanding of conditions in the Clinica Biblica area, five interviews were conducted with neighborhood representatives. Each interview lasted approximately one hour, with participants receiving no payment for their involvement. Furthermore, ten additional interviews were carried out with civil servants, area merchants, drug dealers, and representatives of nongovernmental organizations. Finally, interviews were conducted with ILPES staff members who work with transvestites (i.e., in such programs as Group 2828 and "Priscilla" of the April 5th Movement), along with a number of their clients. Again, no payment was made in return for the participation of the latter groups in the study. In this regard it should also be noted that an ethnographer was retained for a period of three weeks to visit transvestites' "pick-up" areas and to report on any changes that may have occurred in recent years, as well as on present-day social conditions.

Given that the sources of information for this study come from two different periods, particular attention was paid to the task of highlighting the areas of greatest contrast. Data drawn from the 1989 study were used in areas in which there was little or no noticeable change, such as age of sexual initiation, family relationships, friends and lovers, drug use, number of sexual partners, and sexual practices. By contrast, in areas in which the greatest differences presented themselves, material from the 1997 qualitative interviews was used; these include location of work, pay rates in the sex trade, types of lovers and sexual partners, relations with the state, and conceptions of fashion and beauty.

Acknowledgments

I would like to express my gratitude to all those people who have assisted in the preparation of this work. First, to the Research Department at ILPES (Latin American Institute for Health Education and Prevention), especially Dino Starcevic, who undertook much of the research and writing for Chapters 2 and 4. I would also like to thank Mary Gómez and Diana Dávila, who spent long hours proofreading earlier drafts of the manuscript, and Herman Loría, coordinator of the Priscilla Project, an AIDS prevention program for transvestites, who was of great help to our ethnographers and interviewers. Moreover, I must also acknowledge the assistance of Héctor Elizondo who, as coordinator of Group 2828, ILPES's support program for young transvestites, carried out a number of key interviews as well as making several valuable suggestions that have since been incorporated into the final draft of this report. Héctor's knowledge of the day-to-day realities facing transvestites in Costa Rica is unsurpassed; as such he has contributed significantly to the success of this project.

Members of the board of directors of the Clinica Biblica's Neighbors' Association, along with the Governor of San José, Jorge Vargas, have all been very patient and understanding in their dealings with us, providing help as needed and assisting us in the incorporation of their legitimate concerns into the present work. Finally, it must be emphasized that this work could never have been completed without the active support of the transvestite community itself. Not only did they give freely of their time and knowledge, but, more fundamentally, they also opened their hearts and souls to us. In turn, this book forms part of a larger project whose aim is to improve transvestites' living conditions and to provide alternatives and employment opportunities for members of this community.

The contents of this work, including any errors or omissions, are the responsibility of the author alone.

To all, thank you very much.

Introduction

When we began working with the transvestite community in 1989, one of our principal aims was to learn more about transvestites' sexual culture, along with the risk factors associated with the spread of HIV in this population. Another aim was to gather information about this sexual culture in a specifically Latin American context, as a means of filling what is in effect a highly significant gap in the literature. These two concerns remained at the fore as we embarked upon the second set of interviews in 1997. This work, therefore, seeks to analyze the sexual culture and risk factors that place transvestites and their customers at risk of contracting HIV.

Apparently, there has been very little change in the risk factors present over the past seven years. However, by the same token it is clear that very significant changes have occurred in other aspects of participants' lives. This in turn led us to formulate a third objective for our study: the impact of *paqueteo*[1] upon the etiology of sexual orientation. We believe that the latter provides valuable information on the plasticity of sexual orientation, along with the influence of cultural factors in its etiology. As well, it reinforces the view that we should not merely look to a person's genitals and those of his or her partner to determine sexual orientation; any number of cultural, erotic, and emotional factors are equally important in this regard.

Of course, the debate on the determinants of sexual orientation is an old one, with the earliest studies being undertaken in Germany in the mid-nineteenth century. This early work was grounded in an "essentialist" understanding of the origins of homosexuality. Quite simply, it was believed that homosexuality (and, by extension, heterosexuality) was congenital, inherited, and hormonally based. Thus, for writers such as Hirshfeld, homosexuals were intermediate beings—*zwischenstufen* in German—byproducts of "disorders" in the level of estrogens and androgens found in their systems. Men who had an overabundance of female hormones, for example, would develop female souls, while in women the opposite would occur; homosexuality was thus an inversion whereby male bodies were inhabited by female souls, and vice versa. In view of the fact that the onset of homosexuality came at such an early stage of an individual's development, it was believed that there was very little that could be done to alter one's sexual orientation.

However, an opposite position would be taken by subsequent writers, Sigmund Freud most notable among them.[2] For the father of modern psychology, homosexuality was as much the product of cultural factors as it was of genetic predisposition. Although Freud believed that the degree of "passivity" or "activity" in a child was hereditary and that this in turn played an important role in determining sexual orientation, he nonetheless devoted considerable attention to nonconstituent factors: most significantly, interpersonal relations. According to the Viennese doctor, all children go through a phase in which they feel love and desire for their parent of the opposite sex. This phase is usually resolved "successfully" with the acquisition of a heterosexual orientation. However, cultural factors such as possessiveness on the part of the mother, indifference on the part of the father, jealousy among siblings, guilt feelings, and aggression can serve to influence a child's development and potentially engender "deviations," of which homosexuality is just one.

For Freud, the implantation of sexual orientation takes place at such an early phase of development—between three and five years of age—and in such an unconscious manner that, once established, it is almost impossible to change. Thus, he did not believe that psychiatry should be employed for this purpose. However, not all of his followers agreed with him on this point, with some going on to try to "cure" individuals of their so-called "deviation" from heterosexuality. Ferenczi, for example, believed that a homosexual male was in reality a "repressed heterosexual," someone who is both neurotic and "tormented and plagued by obsessions," and as such in need of psychoanalytic intervention.[3] Along similar lines, Bieber, a New York psychiatrist, claimed that homosexuality was so unnatural that it could only be a learned behavior. Moreover, given that it was learned, it could also be "unlearned." In order to do this, he elaborated a series of interventions designed to remedy homosexuality's "causes," that is to say by combating the mother's "aggressiveness" and the father's "passivity."[4]

In turn, the postwar years might be characterized as a period of renaissance for cultural explanations of the causes of homosexuality. However, despite the best efforts of the mainstream psychiatric community, the techniques developed at this time to transform homosexuals into heterosexuals proved incapable of achieving satisfactory results. Few psychiatrists were able to "cure" their patients, despite the application of any number of courses of treatment (or torture?), from aversion therapy to psychoanalysis, from hormone therapy to lobotomy. Not only were they unsuccessful in their attempts to alter sexual orientation, but they also failed to demonstrate, in the numerous laboratory studies undertaken at the time, that homosexuals' mental health or family histories differed from those of nonhomosexuals. In this way, Evelyn Hooker was able to demonstrate that specialists would be unable to judge the sexual orientation of individuals based upon their medical history folders, despite the fact that the men who participated in the study had been given standard "tests" to determine their sexual orientation.[5] Similarly, Weinberg and Hammersmith found no difference in the family histories of heterosexual and homosexual individuals; both groups had the same proportion of "possessive mothers" and "distant fathers."[6] These failures, combined with the gathering momentum of the gay liberation movement, would lead the psychiatric community in 1971 to abandon the position that homosexuality was a pathology in urgent need of treatment.[7]

During the past two decades, however, a number of scientists have again tried to ground homosexuality in biology. Günter Dörner, for one, claimed that a homosexual orientation is the product of hormonal imbalances during pregnancy.[8] Along somewhat different lines, Professor D. F. Swaab[9] contended that a particular area of the hypothalamus, known as the suprachiasmatic region, is "sexually disphormic," that is, it varies according to gender and sexual orientation. In 1991, Simon LeVay[10] discovered yet another nucleus in the hypothalamus (INAH 3) that was thought to be larger in heterosexual men than in either women or homosexual men. However, at the same time, LeVay stressed that, aside from the INAH 3 nucleus, he could find no evidence to support the contentions of Swaab; as far as he was concerned, the hypothalami of men and women were similar. Then, in 1992, Laura Allen would discover another area of the brain, called the anterior commissure (a group of fibers attached to the hypothalamus and connected to the temporal lobes), which differs in size according to gender and sexual orientation.[11] Meanwhile, E. O. Wilson sought to infer cultural behavior patterns from the laws of genetics and the survival of the fittest.[12] In this way, homosexuality was said to be caused by a gene, transmitted from one generation to the next through a process known as "superior enhanced heterozygote adaption." A similar position underlay the work of Hamer and Copeland, who in 1993 discovered a genetic marker (known as Xq28) on the X chromosome that was found in significant numbers of gay brothers.[13]

Needless to say, these scientists all assume that human society comprises discrete groups of homosexual, bisexual, and heterosexual individuals, whose genes, hypothalami, and neuron paths are all readily comparable. However, if this was not the case, their work would instantly lose much of its meaning and significance. What then is one to make of their assumptions?

CULTURAL OR BIOLOGICAL FACTORS?

As one might imagine, any analysis of the sexual culture of Costa Rica's transvestite community underscores the plasticity of sexual orientation and, by extension, calls into question the validity of essentialist assumptions. Most notably, this is seen in the apparent impact of accidental changes in San José's sexual geography upon the likelihood that heterosexual men and women will engage in sexual relations with transvestites. Instead of explanations rooted in hormones, genes, and hypothalami, one might argue that a simple relocation in the working zone of transvestites holds enormous consequences for the sexual lives of heterosexual men and women. In short, we will show how physical space, combined with *paqueteo,* plays a highly significant role in promoting changes in sexual orientation.

We believe that our research also serves to undermine attempts to categorize people according to their sexual orientation. As De Cecco[14] makes clear, by no means should such attempts be based upon patterns of physical activity alone, which is of course typical of essentialist writings. Quite simply, instead of classifying individuals merely on the basis of the genitals of the person with whom they are having sex, one must also take stock of their desires and emotions. After all, it is quite possible to be heterosexual in one's sexual practice but homosexual in one's passions or desires. It was not the aim of our research to create further labels to describe these boundary-crossing individuals, but rather to document their existence and to subvert the simplistic division of people into traditional psychiatric categories.

If one requires proof that these categories are incapable of grasping the complexities of human sexual practices, one need only reflect upon their patent inability to help us answer questions about the main characters in this book. How is one to classify a married heterosexual man who likes to dress as a woman while at home? Or a lesbian who has sexual relations with a transvestite because she likes his masculine eroticism? Or a heterosexual woman who has sexual relations with a transvestite because she is emotionally attracted to him? Are we to consider a transvestite to be heterosexual when he penetrates a woman for money?

BACKGROUND ON TRANSVESTISM

Contemporary conceptions of transvestism originated in the nineteenth century. The phenomenon is as old as civilization itself, with ancient accounts of the practice surviving to the present day, despite the best efforts of Judeo-Christian religions to erase from history any evidence of men and women dressing in clothes belonging to the opposite sex.

Thus, Bullough and Bullough[15] provide ample proof to support the claim that transvestism has been a constant in both the West and East. Jewish leaders condemned it precisely because of its link with the fertility rites of pagan religions, in which noblemen dressed as women would engage in sex with either men or women to guarantee prosperity or a bountiful harvest. In spite of their prohibition, many continued to engage in pagan rituals in the West, including cross-dressing for ceremonial or ritual reasons. Indeed, one might argue that the legacy of these ancient festivities is preserved to the present day in the celebration of Halloween or the Mardi Gras carnival. As well, rituals continue to be practiced, as in the case of Greek funerals and lay festivities, whereby men and women dress themselves in the clothing of the opposite sex.

There is also a long tradition of women in the West who cross-dressed to escape gender restrictions, with Joan of Arc being perhaps the best-known example. Along somewhat different lines, many noblemen in European courts would cross-dress as a means of becoming more attractive to their female counterparts. It is for this reason that transvestism became associated with heterosexual promiscuity.

In Native American culture, there is a long tradition of transvestism embodied in the figure of the "berdache."[16] These were men who cross-dressed and were given the role of healer or political leader. In India, Burma, and Pakistan, individuals who cross-dressed were considered members of a "third sex," with special posts in society being reserved for them. In India's Dhed community, men dress as women and as such are temporarily possessed by goddesses or female demons.[17] Meanwhile, traditional Tahitian culture includes the "mahu," the town homosexual, who was in effect a transsexual who had elected to become an "honorary" woman, garnering respect from the wider community in the process.[18]

HISTORICAL REASONS FOR CROSS-DRESSING

People who cross-dress do so for many different reasons. In Europe, there are many accounts of "libertines" dressing as women to seduce nuns and virgins. A similar ruse was employed by French aristocrats, with one famous example being a king who would cross-dress in order to pass unnoticed into the maids' quarters. Women who cross-dressed for reasons rather more political than sexual: male attire allowed them to travel, work, and live independent lives in an era in which the movement and activities of women were highly circumscribed. In medieval Holland for example, many women dressed as men fought in the armed forces.[19] Similarly, there are hundreds of documented cases of women going to battle in the American Civil War.[20] Others lived religious lives as men and were later canonized as female saints. Some have even suggested that one or two of the medieval popes may have been women in disguise.[21] During the colonial era, many Dutch women were reported to have cross-dressed to travel to their country's overseas territories. Then, once disembarked, they changed attire and married their male immigrant counterparts.[22] Interestingly, a similar phenomenon is reported to have taken place in the Old West of the United States. Women who wished to break free of restrictive gender roles used male dress to live as "passing women" in remote farms or ranches.

In the face of a widespread interdiction in premodern Europe against female employment in the theater or opera, hundreds of men were castrated to play the female parts.[23] Writers such as Ackroyd have noted that the Japanese had a similar tradition as well.[24] Of course, in addition to the reasons outlined above, it is clear that some men cross-dressed because they were what we would now call gay. For them, cross-dressing was a way to attract men at a time when "sodomy" was severely punished.

WHO ARE TODAY'S TRANSVESTITES?

We are in what might be described as a middle-class home in the middle of a San José neighborhood. It has all the conveniences of modern life: color TV, washing machine, microwave oven, and so on. "This is my hair dryer," announces Javier, the home owner. I look at it, but it doesn't really register in my mind, as I'm busy admiring his weight machines instead. "This is my small gym," says Javier, when he realizes what I'm doing. "Are you into weight lifting yourself?" I reply that I like to pump iron, that I find it exhilarating, even though I can tell that he is not really interested in my response. "Well, I like to wash my hair every day and straighten it with this hair dryer. I hate my curls." Clearly, this bodybuilder is more interested in his curls than his muscles.

Javier is a big man. He has well-developed biceps and a muscular body. His chest is large and firm. His buns are as hard as steel. At thirty-two, he is both beautiful and sexy. His face is masculine: Semitic nose, curly black hair (when not straightened), well-defined cheekbones, large white teeth, Mediterranean mouth, and small ears. In short, he is the typically good-looking Costa Rican male that has made this country justly famous. As a foreign diplomat once said to me earnestly, "Costa Rica is better known for its men than its women, though because of machismo, no one will admit it."

Javier sits down on his sofa and asks me straight out: "Do you find me attractive?" "Well, yes," I reply with some embarrassment. He looks at me. "I find it hard to understand how a man could like another man. I have nothing against it, it's just that I can't understand it." "Javier," I respond, "I also find it perplexing that a man like you, married with two children, into sports, can be so fond of the feminine." As I say this, I can't take my eyes off the framed photo, sitting on a table between us, of this hunk along with his wife and two children. "Your wife is very pretty," I tell him. "Yes, she's a very sexy woman," he replies with pride.

The bodybuilder looks at me intently, and I feel he's sizing me up from head to toe before giving me an answer. "Look, Jacobo, I resent having to explain to you something that belongs to me and is mine alone, and that you probably won't get anyway. There are certain things in a man's life that are very private, which no one should ask about, especially a researcher." Javier is right. Why do we think that there is an explanation for every human action? The interview, like the confession, is designed to induce people to reveal their most intimate secrets. Who said that we have to talk about ourselves? Foucault for one abhorred the intrusiveness of priests, teachers, psychiatrists, and researchers into individuals' personal lives, an intrusiveness he identified with the Inquisition and the prison. Nevertheless, as one of his biographers contends, Foucault himself confessed before his death to having wished, while a schoolboy in occupied France, for the extermination of his Jewish classmates.[25]

Javier does not speak, nor do I try to make him. To my surprise, however, he suddenly takes off his shirt, watching all the while the confused look on my face. He shows me his biceps and the fine tufts of curly hair on his chest, his flat stomach without an ounce of fat on it, his long, tanned arms. "This is a macho torso," he tells me. "It has taken me years to develop it." He smiles and winks at me. He is not finished yet. He slowly takes off his jeans, his tight-fitting, beige briefs, his white socks and tennis shoes. He stands stark naked in front of me and still he continues to stare.

I am sweating and I don't know what to say. What is he trying to show me? Where is this leading? I came here today to find a particular sort of man and perhaps I've made a mistake. "Javier," I say softly, "what are you trying to tell me?" I find it difficult to speak when I'm feeling so uncomfortable. I try not to stare at his long dick and large balls, but how can I avoid looking at them when they're right there in front of me? I think about the social taboos that serve to render our bodies off-limits to the stares of others. Why can't we take a good look? Why is this man so intent that I see his genitals and how large they are? Who cares in any case?

The bodybuilder raises himself from the sofa and goes into the kitchen, where he appears to be looking for something. He then disappears into his bedroom, closing the door behind him as he goes in. "What's he doing in there?" I ask myself. We men have very strange relationships with our bedrooms, particularly when we are by ourselves. Masculinity is also about posing for others. When a man is alone in his bedroom, he can become a movie star, a bull-fighter, a model. I hear Javier shouting at me through the wall: "Men are very vain animals. However, the big difference between us and women is that we too admire our bodies when we're alone, when no one can see us, but do not admit it."

The door opens. What the hell is going on? Javier is now in drag, wearing a blond wig, a white satin dress, and pink bloomers. "Now you can ask me whatever the fuck you want," he says in a low voice. Although I try to look cool, I cannot hide my confusion. I knew Javier liked to cross-dress because a transvestite had given me his phone number. I had called him because I was writing an article on heterosexual cross-dressers. We had made the appointment on a day when his wife and children were away. Nevertheless, up until this point I was unsure whether this guy really was a transvestite. I took a deep breath, and started the interview.

When did you start to cross-dress?

I started wearing my sister's underwear when I was six. I would lock myself in the bathroom and try them on. I loved the bright colors, the smell of perfume, the softness of the fabric. When I became a teenager I began to wear bras and then, when I got married, I started to use lipstick.

How do you explain the fact that you like to cross-dress, but are not gay?

I have nothing to explain. I'm simply not queer.

But people think that all transvestites are queer.

Yes, but I like women.

Okay, sure, but aren't you dressed like that in order to attract men?

I might be dressed as a woman, but I don't do it to turn you on.

Then why do you do it?

It's a physical need. I like to wear women's clothes, and put on this little show for myself. I love the feel of satin against my cock, the way a bra envelops my breasts, or the way lipstick looks on my mouth.

When you think about having sex with someone, don't you see a man in front of you?

Not at all. I think about a woman. I imagine that we've met at a party and she does not know that I'm a man. I imagine that she invites me to stay over at her place, thinking that I'm just a girlfriend. Once in the bedroom, I turn off the lights and ask if she minds if we sleep together. She suspects nothing. She says yes of course, and gets into bed wearing only her underwear. I ask her if she's ever been in bed with a woman before. She says no, but that she doesn't mind trying it out. I tell her that I am a lesbian and that I would like to kiss her. Once she's let herself be kissed, I fondle her and make her feel the way that only a man can make a woman feel. Finally she realizes that she's in bed with a man, and lets me penetrate her.

But Javier, why the need to cross-dress?

Because the clothes turn me on. It gives me this weird erotic desire. It lets me think in a different way. I just love how the clothes feel on me.

Does your wife know that you cross-dress?

She wouldn't understand. She's very conservative. She likes the macho image I project, and I don't want to disappoint her.

THE MAJORITY OF TRANSVESTITES
ARE HETEROSEXUAL

Most cross-dressers are in fact heterosexual. In other words, it is not only gay men who seek to act in ways that society defines as typically "female"; such activity transcends sexual orientation. Recent studies have shown that this is the case historically as well, with homo-, bi-, hetero-, and asexual men engaging in the practice at various times and places. However, the key difference between gay and straight transvestites is that the latter are usually far more reserved. As Feinbloom has shown, the incidence of transvestism among heterosexual men is far more widespread than is typically believed.[26]

Thus, as has been made clear, although cross-dressing is associated with all sexual orientations, heterosexual cross-dressers do not share with their gay counterparts any of the same feelings toward men. Indeed, many straight cross-dressers are as homophobic as any other heterosexual man:

> Can somebody sincerely place a married man with three children, who lives on a farm, who voted for Nixon, who fought in World War II, who goes to mass on Sundays, who loves sports cars and who expresses his femininity in the sanctity of his home, in the same category of faggot and child molester?[27]

It should be noted that even though heterosexual transvestites have set up larger organizations in the United States than is the case for gay cross-dressers, the mainstream news media, in either the United States or Costa Rica, refuses to expose them. Thus, as Javier puts it, "You will never read in conservative Costa Rican papers that one of their most honorable citizens is a transvestite, or that such and such literary critic likes to wear a bra."

Charles Prince, founder of the Society for Personal Expression in the 1960s, and known today as Virginia Prince, has demonstrated conclusively that transvestism is mainly a heterosexual phenomenon. His organization now has hundreds of chapters across the United States. The majority of its members are heterosexual men, like Prince himself, who is described on the dust jacket of one of his books as follows:

. . . raised as a normal kid, he became a university athlete, obtained his PhD in science, married twice, fathered a child and founded and became President for 18 years of his own corporation. Finally, after his second divorce and the sale of his business, he decided to do permanently what he had been doing occasionally throughout his adult life: dress as a woman.[28]

In Costa Rica, the transvestite community is far less visible than it is in the United States. For example, it took months to make contact with a man like Javier. Here, straight cross-dressers do not form umbrella organizations. They do not have established meeting places, nor do they walk the streets in drag in the way that some gay transvestites do. In short, they remain as closeted as many married homosexual men.

"Javier, have you ever met anyone like yourself?" I once asked him. "No," he answered, going on to explain that he had never told his secret to any of his friends, and that he only talks about it with homosexual transvestites. "Sometimes I look for a transvestite, and bring him home just to sit down and talk to him." However, he went on to assure me that "I could never imagine having sex with him. I don't like drag queens."

Looking at this man who is dressed like a woman, I involuntarily think that there must be something wrong with him. Like most Costa Ricans, I've been taught from a very early age to see sexuality in strictly dualistic terms: there are only two sexes and only two genders. But Javier has shown me that in truth things are somewhat more complex. "Why do you have to see things only in black and white?" he asked me. "Who told you that a man who dresses as a woman must automatically cease to be attracted to women?" Javier is right. I have never understood why it is that we are so proud of our country's political pluralism, yet tolerate nothing of the sort in the sexual realm. If we accept that there are people of the right, left, and center, that there are people who are anarchist or fascist, evangelical or atheist, why can't we accept the existence of a similar diversity in matters of sexuality?

CONTEMPORARY ETIOLOGY OF TRANSVESTISM

According to John Money,[29] gender emerges through a learning process, with cultural factors having a large impact upon its particular etiology. Boys and girls learn gender through prevailing stereotypes. In short, each child internalizes the role assigned to his or her gender within a given cultural context. However, by the same token Money argues that children are also taught how to "talk" in the other gender's language, garnering in this way a form of sexual bilingualism. Notwithstanding the latter, children are made constantly aware of the fact that, if they are to be accepted as normal in society, they must refrain from speaking the language of the other gender.

For some reason as yet unknown, men such as Javier, be they gay or straight, have not learned this lesson, and continue to speak the feminine language throughout their lives.

Some psychoanalysts believe that this is due to an arrested sexual development whereby the child does not resolve successfully his or her sexual identification with the parent of the opposite sex.[30] Stoller summarizes the various hypotheses used to explain it thus: (1) an unconscious desire on the part of the mother to feminize the child; (2) the father acts either as an accomplice to the mother or else distances himself from the child; (3) the boy fears castration and compensates for this by fantasizing about becoming a "phallic" woman; and (4) transvestism becomes a way of sexually identifying with the female, without actually becoming female oneself. Thus, when the child cross-dresses, he keeps his penis, which reminds him that he is still a man.[31]

However, it should be noted that studies which have attempted to link transvestism, or homosexuality for that matter, with a specific family history have consistently failed to do so in a convincing manner; the families of homosexuals are no different from those of heterosexuals.[32] There is no conclusive evidence to suggest that sexual orientation is the product of hormonal imbalances. No scientist has been able to prove that transvestism is a pathology, or that those who practice it suffer from a "mental disorder."

CHILDHOOD BEGINNINGS

Transvestites believe that their desire to cross-dress is natural and that, as such, it does no harm to society at large. They are also aware that this desire manifested itself from a very early age (three to five years is typical), long before they were in a position to make a conscious decision about it.

> I have been a transvestite since I was a little boy. I had this strong sense that I was more girl than boy, that it was already in my system. Each one of us is like that. It's about time that people accept us; I would like to have more freedom and lead a normal life. If there was a transvestites' organization in this country, I would join it immediately. (Maria)

> I wanted to be a girl ever since I was born. I would hide my sisters' clothes and dolls in order to play with them later by myself. I did it because I loved dressing as a girl and I still want to do it. (Lidia)

As one might imagine, these boys faced tremendous pressure from those who wanted to "normalize" them. Marcella remembers her stepfather burning her underwear and skirts to force her to be a "man." Kristina was subjected to terrible punishment when caught wearing makeup: "My aunt would beat the hell out of me every time she found me with lipstick or makeup in my bathroom." Anna Karenina was locked in her room for days on end whenever her grandmother caught her in the closet playing with her clothes. Miriam's family would strike her when they caught her singing in feminine voice.

However, in spite of what was done to dissuade them, these children continued to identify with the female. Of course, this is not to say that the punishments meted out had no effect; one need only consider all those gay or straight men who today, as adults, continue to practice transvestism in secret. Transvestites who allow themselves to be seen in public may be more bold or daring in their conviction, but they are by no means the only ones.

For a researcher, the central problem with men such as Javier is that they are inaccessible and thus, if one is to gain an understanding of the transvestites' world, one can only do so through the eyes of those who are homosexual and out of the closet. Perhaps in the not-so-distant future, more closet cross-dressers such as Javier will allow us to interview them, permitting us in the process to compare their experiences with those of transvestites involved in the sex trade. This in turn would allow us to gain a more balanced vision of cross-dressing culture. As Javier himself put it, "We transvestites form a community. Some of us like women, some like men, but all of us love to dress as women."

Chapter 1

Expulsion from Eden

FERNANDO

Fernando waits until his mother is out visiting a friend. Once he is sure that she's gone, he walks into his sister's room and picks out a dress from her closet. It is made of white cotton with a pattern of yellow flowers. The twelve-year-old boy proceeds to put on his mother's wig, along with some lipstick and makeup, and is suddenly transformed into a pretty fifteen-year-old girl, singing and dancing in front of the mirror: "I saw a plane, a train, and a beautiful ship in the sea . . . " In a stroke, Fernando has shed his own persona and become Mona Bell, his favorite Chilean singer. He does not know why it happens; only that he has been doing it for as long as he can remember and that he has not told anyone his secret—that he feels like a girl and loves to dress as one.

Today, however, is not to be like all the other days. His mother has forgotten her change purse and Fernando, singing and dancing in his sister's bedroom, is not aware of her return. Suddenly, Fernando's mother is standing before him. "But miss, who are you?" she asks in astonishment, not realizing at first that it is her son. For Fernando, time has stopped. Mother and son stare at each other across the room, each feeling like a stranger to the other. Then, as it slowly begins to dawn on her, her astonishment turns to anger. "But it's you!" she screams. "How can you do this to me?" As the mother starts to strike her son across the face, the only words Fernando can think to say are "Mama, forgive me, forgive me!"

From this day on, things will never be the same. In the evening, as soon as Fernando's stepfather comes home from work, his mother tells him what happened. "Imagine how I felt when I saw him dressed like that, singing like a queer in front of the mirror. I thought I'd raised him to be a man." "Well, I think you've always pampered the boy too much," opines the stepfather. "It's no wonder he's turned out to be such a pansy." He has no doubt about what is needed here, and leaves the room to seek Fernando. He finds him in his bedroom, sobbing in shame and fear. There is nowhere for Fernando to hide. "Come here, you fucking queer, I'm gonna teach you to be a man. I'm gonna beat the woman out of your fucking body. You don't know how much you've hurt your mother, you little faggot!" The man jumps all over the boy, hitting him in his face, his mouth, his legs, his arms. Blood oozes from the boy's wounds. His lips are bloody red. The stepfather yells at him again: "You goddamn queer, you're going to become a man whether you want to or not!"

Three years have gone by. Fernando has never again dressed like a girl. He has never had the chance. Whenever his mother goes out, she locks him in the house. She spies on his friends, and forbids him to go out in the evening with other boys. On weekends, she never lets him out of her sight. As for the stepfather, even though he has not raised the topic again, his attitude toward the boy has changed; no longer does he kiss or hug him. Fernando's only close relationship is with his sister, though she is too involved with her own problems to be of much help to him.

One day at school Fernando meets a new classmate. They become friends and eventually the boy invites him home. Fernando is attracted to him, as he seems both masculine and daring. Once at his house, the boy leads him into his bedroom, where he suggests that they play a game of poker. However, the rules say that whoever loses must take off an article of clothing, and soon Fernando, who is not a good poker player, is almost naked.

When he has only his briefs left to lose, his friend takes out a bra and puts it on him, and then proceeds to paint his lips red. Then he reaches into an open drawer, pulls out a woman's blouse, and asks Fernando to put it on. Fernando is in a state of shock; he feels as though someone has just discovered his most intimate secret, a secret that should never have been revealed. But at the same time it feels so right, so good, as though Mona Bell had returned and Fernando was no longer Fernando. The boy kisses him passionately and says,

"You'll never be Fernando for me again. From now on I'll always think of you as my girlfriend."

The next day Fernando is wracked by an overpowering sense of guilt. He decides to seek help from the parish priest: "Father, I have sinned." "Tell me everything, Fernando," the priest replies. "In what way have you sinned?" Fernando feels that he can trust him—after all, he is another young man—and so tells him what happened:

Father, I feel attracted to one of my classmates.

What do you mean by "feeling attracted"? Have you ever had carnal contact with him?

Yes, Father. He's kissed me on the mouth and we've been in bed together.

What else have you done? I need to know everything.

We made love, as they say.

Did you engage in sexual intercourse?

What does "intercourse" mean?

Did he fuck you?

Yes, Father. I was very confused.

Did you enjoy it? Did you feel pleasure?

A little bit. It hurt a lot in the beginning.

Have you sinned again?

Only twice.

Do you always play the role of woman with him?

How did you know that I dress as a woman?

No, I'm asking if he fucked you again. Do you dress up as a woman?

Yes, Father. Is that also a sin?

Of course! Both acts are frowned upon by God. The Bible forbids homosexuality, which is deemed to be an abominable sin. The Gospel also condemns men who dress up as women, and those who try to change their sex. You're a man and as such you mustn't let yourself be used as a whore. Remember Christ told Mary Magdalene that she should cease her sinful acts. Doing what you're doing is unacceptable. In fact, it's a very serious crime.

But what am I to do? Ever since I was a little boy I've dressed up in girls' clothing. I feel like I should have been a girl myself.

No! You cannot continue doing this. Aren't you a normal man? Do you have any physical problems, like a hormone imbalance or something?

No, I don't think so. But I feel like a woman, and this is something I've always felt.

Let me take a look at you to see if you're normally developed. Pull down your pants so that I can see your genitals. Mmmm, your penis is rather small; no wonder you feel like a girl. Does it feel nice if I touch you? Where exactly? Show me how your friend kissed you. I will let you see my penis so that you can compare. Do you see what I mean? Mine is quite a bit bigger than yours. Was your friend's this large?

Yes, Father. It was about the size of yours.

Well, whenever you feel the urge to dress like a woman or have sex with a man, I want you to come to me and I will let you touch my penis. This will help to eliminate your desire. By touching mine yours will also begin to grow. Don't worry! We're not doing anything bad, I'm merely trying to set you on the right path. I will now do what your friend did, in order to show you that you do not really like how it feels. It's a sort of exorcism to beat the devil out of you. Remember, you mustn't talk about this with anyone. We are in confession and this is strictly between you and I. Now turn around and I will start.

After this "spiritual" experience, Fernando is more confused than ever. Years later, he will realize that the priest had sexually abused him. Nevertheless, he feels so guilty that he drops his relationship with his classmate, feeling as though Mona Bell has died and there is no longer anywhere safe for him to go where he can let himself be transformed into his idol.

He begins to look for help from other boys who are like him. One night, one of them invites him to a drag party. He feels wonderful! Once again, he can be the person he wants to be. That night, for the first time, he decides to walk the streets in drag and is picked up by a man near the Clinica Biblica. This man, a lawyer, turns out to be his first customer, and later helps him move out of his house. He never returns home again.

EARLY AWARENESS

Fernando, like other transvestites, is part of a group of boys who realized very early in their lives that they were different from most of their friends and classmates. In short, their femininity set them apart from others in their peer group.

> I started dressing up as a girl when I was very small. The men's clothes that my father bought me, I threw them in the river. I was so wild that I would go to school dressed like a girl. My classmates would throw stones at me and my teachers would send me home because wearing such clothes was forbidden. (Marlene)

Once their male classmates realized that these boys were different, they would start to tease and harass them, strengthening their self-awareness in the process. For this reason, transvestites tend to become aware of their homosexuality much earlier than other gay men do (the average age for the former is nine and a half, compared with twelve years for the latter) (see Table 1.1). They tend to undergo sexual initiation at an earlier age as well.

> I came out at seventeen, though men were taking advantage of me since I was a little boy: the baker, the store owner, the butcher. . . . They can see that you're effeminate and so they start giving you candy so that they can fondle you, they give you presents so that they can have you. (Elisa)

TABLE 1.1. Age of Sexual Initiation and Age of First Orgasm (Percent)

Variable	Gay	Transvestite sex-trade workers
(N)	(162)	(22)
Total	100	100
Average age at which one felt sexually different	12.3	9.5
Average age of first orgasm	12.6	12.2
With whom did one have one's first orgasm?		
Total	100	100
Alone	67.3	18.2
Wet dream	4.3	—
Other male	24.1	81.8
Woman (girl)	2.5	—
Other	1.9	—
Was one's sexuality defined through this experience?		
Total	100	100
Yes	22.8	45.5
No	77.2	54.5

Source: Jacobo Schifter and Johnny Madrigal, *Hombres que Aman Hombres,* San José, Costa Rica, ILEP-SIDA, 1992.

Katrina was routinely stalked by men, and almost raped at the age of ten.

One day this man came along and told me that I was a beautiful boy. He followed me, and then took a gun out and said that he would kill me unless I had sex with him. He took me to a well-known dance club and forced me to go under the stage with him. He pulled down his pants and put his mouth over mine so that I couldn't scream. "I'm going to do what I want to you," he said. But a bouncer heard the commotion and rescued me.

Roxana was not so lucky. Her sexual initiation took place at the age of seven, when three men forced themselves on her: "I was raped by three guys from Guadalupe [a district in San José]. I still see them every day in my neighborhood."

Transvestites' sexual initiation usually takes place with men much older than themselves (average age 22.6), most of whom are also friends or acquaintances (in 68 percent of the cases). It should be noted that this tendency to experience sexual initiation with a man much older than oneself is far more marked among transvestites than it is among other gay men. Katrina's is a representative case:

> My family had a gay friend who came to visit us. He was twenty-seven years old and very big. He always had a thing for me. If my mother went out for a while, he would ask me to sit on his lap and then he would start fondling me. One day, when the two of us were at home alone, he chased me all over the house, took my clothes off, and then put his penis between my legs. "Stick your butt out," he said to me, "so that I can come on your little balls."

However, in this regard it should be noted that, as is the case with other gay men in Costa Rica, although sexual initiation typically occurs with an older man (73 percent of the cases), it is for the most part (77 percent) consensual in nature (see Table 1.2).

Among those surveyed, outright force was used in only 4 percent of the cases. Leticia's experience in this regard is typical:

> My first sexual experience was at age seven when I was raped. I was sent to get some milk and, when I was crossing the river, some guy raped me. He forced himself into me. I remember feeling that I couldn't tell anyone. I felt as though I had died. I still see this man around. I hate him. I would never be able to have sex with him.

Sexual contact between effeminate boys and older men is common in Latin America. Witham and Mathy[1] argue that it is the product of Latin culture's tolerance for this type of behavior. In sharp contrast with Anglo-Saxon sexual mores, such relations are not perceived as homosexual.

TABLE 1.2. Data on Respondents' First True Sexual Relationship with a Man (Percent)

Variable	Gay	Transvestite sex-trade workers
(N)	(162)	(22)
Total	100	100
Average age of first sexual relationship with a man	15.9	12.2
Average age of partner in first sexual relationship	22.2	22.6
Who was this partner?		
Total	100	100
Friend, acquaintance	67.3	68.2
Lover, sexual partner	8.6	4.2
Teacher	2.5	—
Unknown	11.1	—
Prostitute	0.6	4.5
Rape	1.9	4.5
Incest	0.6	—
Other	7.5	18.1
Place where first sexual relationship took place . . .		
Total		
Place of residence	100	100
Residence of friend	16.7	9.1
School	40.7	31.8
College	2.5	—
Open air site	3.1	4.5
Enclosed site	15.4	36.4
Hotel	1.6	—
Other	9.3	4.5
	10.5	13.6
Identity of initiator . . .		
Total	100	100
Respondent	22.8	18.2
Partner	66.7	72.7
Other	10.5	9.1
Was the relationship something one had wished for previously?		
Total	100	100
Yes	69.8	77.3
No	13.6	22.7
Not sure	16.7	—
Sexual activities undertaken during first sexual relationship . . .		
Masturbation	75.9	50.0
Oral sex	59.9	50.0
Anal sex	57.4	77.3
Sexual games	88.9	81.8

Source: Jacobo Schifter and Johnny Madrigal, *Hombres que Aman Hombres,* San José, Costa Rica, ILEP-SIDA, 1992.

What might have happened had Fernando's story turned out differently? Let us try to imagine a different outcome:

> Fernando is singing in his sister's bedroom and hears a noise in the hallway. He knows his mother is back, but doesn't have enough time to change. "Fernando, is that you singing in there?" his mother asks. "Yes, Mama, but don't come into the room." Ignoring him, she comes in anyway, and sees him in drag. "But Fernando, don't you think your sister's clothes look awful on you?" she asks him. "I don't mind it if you want to dress in women's clothes, but at least try do it with some style." Fernando is taken aback. "Aren't you mad at me?" he exclaims. "Not at all. So long as you don't do it in front of your macho stepfather, there's nothing to worry about."

Although neither mother nor child can explain exactly what is happening, the line of communication is not broken. Thus, the door is left open to discuss alternative ways of dealing with something that society disapproves of. Had Fernando been allowed to dress up occasionally at home, perhaps he would not have ended up as a prostitute on the street. Or perhaps he would have anyway. Nevertheless, he would have had the opportunity at least to try to resolve the issues he was facing without being forced out of his home, as happens so often with young transvestites.

Chapter 2

From Toads to Queens

José is a twenty-seven-year-old South American man who came to Costa Rica to escape poverty at home. He is tall, thin, brown-skinned, effeminate, and homely. His eyes are attractive but too large for his face. His lips are full and his hair curly. His voice is high, his hands thin, and his nose slightly turned up. As a man he is not especially attractive. He is not very popular at gay bars and seldom goes to them. Nevertheless, José is also Pepa, who happens to be one of the most sought-after transvestites in San José. As a woman, his body is stunning. His curved hips make him look like Tina Turner. When he wears tight lycra, one would think he is Grace Jones. A short wig makes him look like Oprah. His painted lips remind one of Whitney Houston. And, when he is wearing mascara, his eyes are those of Sophia Loren. As a hooker, José gets everyone's attention. He also undergoes something of a personality change. He becomes hot and fiery, capable of picking up any man on the street. "Being transformed into a princess is every transvestite's dream," he asserts. "Being a princess means looking radiant, turning yourself into an attractive woman."

CREATING THE MAGIC

"Projecting an image" is a phrase that tells us a lot about the transvestite's world, and though few would bother to probe its conceptual basis, everyone knows its meaning: in short, that cross-dressing is about "fantasy, enchantment, and dreams" and that it involves, in the final analysis, the transformation of the unreal into the real.

Cross-dressers invest most of their money in their bodies, though they themselves do not perceive it that way. Clothes, makeup, wigs, and accessories constitute the bulk of this investment.

The majority of transvestites own three wardrobes: for home; for work (prostitution); and for drag shows, parties, or discos. Work dress tends to be simple and sexy; though it must attract customers, it must not be a hindrance when running away from the police or other predators. Outfits worn at drag shows and the like tend to be more fancy, inspired by the gowns of Hollywood stars and covered with feathers, bangles, and tropical bouquets. Finally, clothes worn at home are generally utilitarian and androgynous, without any strong statement regarding the wearer's sexual identity. For instance, when Miriam goes home after work and becomes Hugo, he dresses in clothes that are neither overtly male nor female in appearance; he likes to play with colors, cuts, and accessories in ways that cut across dominant patterns of sex typing. Duquesa and Alba, on the other hand, tend to dress in men's clothes, though at the same time keeping their hair long and nails painted red. Corinthia, meanwhile, always dresses in drag.

Duquesa's work wardrobe includes several collections, mostly black and white, though all of them, she assured us, "bring her luck." Her black work outfits are short, tight, and "not too pretty," since her aim is to be "picked up," rather than "admired." "These gowns are made especially for me by my seamstress. There's also a store I go to where they will make clothes for me at very short notice," she said with pride.

However, when it comes to shoes, accessories, or nightgowns, she buys them at regular stores. For example, most of Duquesa's shoes were bought either at the San Pedro Mall (in San José) or in shoe stores such as Lazo or Clasico (which specialize in high heels and leather boots). She finds these are generally too expensive for daily use: "It's not worth my while to wear boots that cost me seventeen thousand colones [roughly U.S. $70] for a client who's only paying five thousand [U.S. $20]."

Alba, by contrast, tends to make her clothes, especially those that she wears on the street. "I love to wear minis and dresses that are tight-fitting, because I find I look better in them," she said. "Drag queens are tacky, and not even the hookers wear stuff that is so indecent, but the johns love it." One evening she went out wearing only a thong, boots, and a hat, covering herself with a long coat. She also has clothes that she only wears around the house, along with special outfits for parties and other occasions. The latter are bought in fancy boutiques where she admits to "spending a fortune" on them.

As for Corinthia, avoiding complications is her main priority. She makes some of her dresses herself; others she buys from a seamstress. "It's not expensive that I want, but rather light, almost miniature. People sometimes say that my dresses are so light that they probably don't even need hangers," she said with a smile. Miriam is just the opposite; she has a special designer who has been making all of her clothes for the past five years. "She did not mind that I turned into a drag queen," she said. "She has these beautiful magazines where I get ideas for gowns. I love to copy Calvin Klein and Christian Dior." Her casual outfits are also made for her. "I'm finished with boutiques," as she put it.

This is not to say that she would never enter an expensive boutique. From time to time she will go in, try on a dress that she likes, and then later take the pattern to her seamstress:

> I went to this boutique called Sheloky in San José and tried on this dress that was eighty thousand colones [U.S. $330] before taxes. I then copied the design from the model in the window display and took it to my seamstress. From her, I got the dress for only twenty-two thousand colones, since I cut her husband and children's hair and she's very fond of me.

Miriam's other passion is perfume: "They're my weakness. I just can't stop myself. . . . I'd even trade a man for an expensive bottle of perfume." She has invested as much as 200,000 colones (U.S. $700) in an expensive name such as Cartier or Elizabeth Taylor's "Black Pearls." She is proud of the impact her perfume has had on her work. She often challenges her clients to guess what she is wearing and, as she herself emphasized, "I've never lost a client because he feels suffocated by cheap perfume."

Silvester Atelier is the owner of Gipsy International, a store in the Clinica Biblica neighborhood that caters to transvestites and showgirls through its line of extravagant dresses and vaudeville accessories. Originally, he had thought that most of his clients would be transvestites, but soon discovered that this was not to be the case: "Transvestites generally don't have the money to buy my gowns. Sometimes we will sell one or two outfits to a transvestite, or even make one for her, but this is not common."

Along with clothes and perfume, makeup is another indispensable element in the creation of the illusion of femininity among transvestites. Alba, Corinthia, and Duquesa use little, restricting themselves to base, powder, lipstick, and nail polish. Miriam, on the other hand, makes regular use of a wide assortment of skin products, a reflection of her fear of wrinkles and aging: "I invest a lot of money in my skin because I tend not to sleep well and all this sexual activity is very draining. I live for the moment, and always ejaculate because I love my work, and all the more so if my client is somebody I like." She only buys name brands such as Lancôme, Payot, and Estée Lauder, and has upon occasion purchased eyelid repair cream for 32,000 colones, moisturizer for 22,000 colones and, in one case in particular, considered buying (though in the end she did not) a Swiss skin care kit for nearly 400,000 colones (U.S. $1,632).

Most transvestites buy their makeup in boutiques or drugstores. "I buy in drugstores without any problems," reports Miriam. "I have no qualms about going in and asking for makeup. I'll even put it on in front of the salesperson. The ones who do have problems are usually men. Women tend to be more tolerant."

Wigs are the final element in the creation of the transvestite's image, though in recent years there has been a movement away from them, as long hair for men becomes increasingly acceptable in Costa Rican society. For example, Alba and Duquesa's medium-long hair could be that of either a man or a woman. Corinthia, on the other hand, wears her hair extremely long. "Wigs are uncomfortable and hot," reports Miriam, "though some queens' hair is so burnt or kinky that they need to wear wigs or *zorros*, a sort of detachable ponytail."

Wigs and *zorros* are bought at hairdresser salons, some of which cater exclusively to transvestites. As Duquesa put it, "Any time you see a ponytail hanging in a hairdresser's window you know that they serve transvestites." The cost of wigs varies according to the type of hair. If it is synthetic one can expect to pay about 5,000 colones; if it is natural it can cost up to ten times that amount.

Hormones and Padding

Stuffing is another trick used by transvestites. If a man is thin, without hips and curves, one remedy is to apply padding in the appropriate places. The padding can be of various materials, including toilet paper, foam, and even clothing. Lucretia, for example, fills her bra with handkerchiefs. Maria wears ten pairs of panties, one on top of the other, to give herself "wonderful hips." Belly uses foam to increase the size of her bum and to create what she calls "delicious legs." Of course, these tricks only serve to underscore Laura's observation that the stunning bodies which some transvestites appear to have are in fact nothing more than an illusion. As she noted, "One night I went to bed with a client who started to complain after realizing that I was flatter than a tortilla. I told him that most Hollywood stars have silicone implants in their tits. But the guy responded by saying, 'Yeah, but at least those women take their tits to bed with them, while you leave yours on the floor.'"

One area that remains virtually unexplored in Costa Rica is transvestites' use of hormones, typically to "feminize" the body: to develop breasts, change the pitch of one's voice, or increase the amount of fatty tissue around the hips. In Costa Rica, these drugs can be bought without a prescription in any drugstore, though in some cases doctors or clients who are doctors will prescribe them. According to Pablo Soto, a physician working with ILPES, the most commonly used drugs include an injected form of estrogen, Depo-Provera, which they buy in the black market, or simply "whatever they think will work. It's hard to know what the long-term effects of indiscriminate hormone use are, though whatever is happening to their bodies is hidden from us now."

However, it is clear that hormone use does generate significant changes in an individual's appearance. As Herman Loria, coordinator of a support program for transvestites at ILPES, stressed, the physical transformation is such that it often poses problems for them when they go out in public: "If they go out dressed as men, their female characteristics leave them open to harassment; if they go out dressed as women, they risk being beaten up."

CHOOSING A GENDER

For individuals living on the margins of transgenderism, undertaking such everyday tasks as shopping can be quite challenging, with masculine and feminine principles achieving dominance at particular moments in space and time. For example, transvestites tend to act and feel feminine when they are shopping for clothes. However, when they are ready to pay for the outfits they have selected, their poise and voice often change to that of a man. In other words, the single act of shopping is suffused by a range of gender stereotypes: deciding is feminine, buying is masculine. In short, transvestites appear to be more aware than most of us of the profoundly gendered nature of our words and speech patterns.[1] "Queens put on these mini-acts more than most people," explained Katrina. "We make a show of each word in terms of its masculinity or femininity. We are aware that each word is gendered." As one might imagine, this performance garners a strong reaction among salespeople, who respond with hostility or amused friendliness, but never indifference.

Alba tends to patronize regular stores, where she must sometimes contend with hostility or salespeople's outright refusal to serve her. On one occasion, a staff member told her, "Lady, we do not cater to women with balls. If you leave your balls at the door, we'll be happy to serve you." In response, she took some money out of her purse and rubbed it in his face: "I am not a thief, goddamn it, but a paying customer. The only balls that matter are the zeroes in these bills." Miriam is no less aggressive: "I go into a boutique and try on all the dresses. I have a right to do so. The employees sometimes panic and stand there with their mouths hanging open. But if they're not happy with me, I'll throw the dress in their face and leave. Another trick is to pee in the dress while trying it on. 'I'm sorry,' I tell the lady, 'but I'm incontinent today.'" Duquesa, meanwhile, prefers to act butch and manlike when shopping:

> I become very masculine when I'm shopping. I make my eye-brows thicker, I put grease in my hair, take off the nail polish and walk like a man. I usually go and buy men's clothes. Once in a while though, I'll see a woman's dress I like and start to act like a queen so that the saleslady gets the idea and asks if I want to try it on.

Duquesa has an even better solution to the problem of homophobic salespeople: "I only go where people know me. These stores are gay-friendly and do their best to please you. Only once did I get a salesman who refused to show me some women's clothes. I reported him to the owner and he was fired." Esmeralda reported being sent similarly mixed signals by retail personnel. On one occasion when she was shopping for women's shoes in San Pedro Mall, she was told, "Look, honey, try them on if you want to. We're open-minded here." Nevertheless, she has also been informed by other sales staff at the mall that "We don't sell to queers in this store."

EXPRESSING SEPARATE PERSONALITIES

Of course, creating an image is more than simply wearing women's clothes. It has to do with wanting to be someone special. In this way, José and Pepa are two different people who happen to share the same body, with one being more glamorous, more exciting than the other. At different times of the day, in certain places, José continues to exist. In his world, he is a soft-spoken professional whom people like but nothing more. As a woman, Pepa awakens yearning. Looking beautiful and being courted by men who take her out for dancing, dinners, and lovemaking in expensive hotels are the things she loves best: "It makes me happy when I see the men lusting and salivating over me."

Some psychiatrists would argue that individuals who aspire to more than one personality are mentally ill. Hollywood movie producers have reinforced this view by portraying those with multiple personalities in highly distorted terms. Obvious examples include *The Silence of the Lambs,* in which a transsexual psychopath fashions a dress out of women's skin, and *Sybil,* a movie in which transvestites are depicted as nothing other than the inevitable by-product of sexual abuse. However, notwithstanding the dominant view, it is clear that we all have multiple personalities and change our characters many times in a given day. Consider, for instance, the person who goes to mass in the morning and applauds the sermon condemning adulterers, yet in the afternoon is party to a clandestine affair of his own. Or the politician who launches a crusade against corruption while avoiding paying taxes himself. In both cases, the individual in question may be seen as having two faces, one public, one private.

Of course, many would simply label such behavior hypocritical, yet one would be better served by seeing the latter as varying manifestations of a condition known as multiple personality disorder. Who would argue that we are the same person at ten, twenty, or fifty years of age? The changes that take place in a person over his or her lifetime are no less significant than those which drive someone else to wear boxer shorts one day and bloomers the next.

It is not clear when it began to be taken for granted in the West that one must have a unified personality to be seen as normal. Freud of course contributed when he theorized that the path to a "normal" heterosexual existence can only be reached by passing through a number of discrete psychological stages.[2] Be this as it may, the little work that has been produced on the subject cannot lead anyone to the conclusion that cross-dressing makes one either healthier or sicker.[3] In short, transvestites dress as women for numerous reasons, not all linked to the desire to be sexually attractive to men. For example, homosexual cross-dressers go in drag to gay bars where the men have no interest in them. Others wear women's clothes at home, when no one else can see them. For many, pleasure is derived simply from the acquisition of makeup, wigs, jewelry, and accessories. As Pepa would argue, transvestites aspire to a different state of being.

FEELING LIKE A PRINCESS

The following dialogue comes from an interview with Pepa/José.

There are people who would say that you're mentally ill. How would you respond to that?

I really enjoy what I do. As well, I'm a productive person, and I like my work as a journalist. I'm not doing anything wrong by cross-dressing. When people criticize me, most do so less for dressing in drag and more for doing what I want. Of course, the reality is that we all have deep, hidden desires to do crazy things, but we're generally too scared to actually go ahead and do them. Some people would like to make love stark naked on a beach but are too scared to do so. Others dream about stealing a whole bunch of money but are afraid of being caught. Thus, when people see a transvestite, they're angry and jealous that here's somebody who has the guts to do what he wants and doesn't care what society thinks. This is what triggers the anger more than anything. They feel that we've got the balls to do what is forbidden. This is why they call us sick, perverts, criminals. What's wrong with a man wearing women's clothes? Who said that pink is feminine and blue is masculine? That's all bullshit. In Scotland, men wear skirts and it's seen as normal. Priests go around in these long black dresses and no one says anything. Why is it that a monsignor can dress in pink and I can't?

But you have to hide from people. You can't be Pepa and José at the same time.

I can't be both because of prejudice. Nonetheless, there are people who know both faces.

What do you feel when you are José?

I feel like anyone else, whereas with Pepa it's different.

How do you mean?

When I'm dressed as a woman I have another personality. I am happier, sexier, more seductive. I feel more sure of myself and can attract straight men who are looking for a woman. It's a different relationship. We talk about different things and I even feel my body temperature is different. However, one doesn't dress like a woman only to attract a man. Not at all! One does it because one wants to experiment with something new, get into one's feminine side, and be emotional, soft, and sexy. One wants to look pretty. Of course, straight men also have these tendencies but they're afraid of letting them out, and so they look for drag queens so that they can vicariously experience what it's like to be a woman. With us, they can let themselves explore their feminine side. They're so cowardly and frustrated!

Do you think transvestism makes people react to you differently?

Of course. In the first place, when I dress like a woman, people respond to me as though I really were one. Even my friends, who know that I'm a man, when they see me wearing a dress they don't talk to me like they usually do. They are softer and more considerate. They light my cigarette for me or help me down the stairs. These are learned reactions that we all have when we are with a woman. My clients are straight men. They'd never dream of having sex with a man. But they see me as a woman. They treat me differently, kinder and more gently than a gay man would. They whisper romantic stuff into my ear, and they're more careful when they're having sex with you.

What do you feel when you take off your makeup and wig and become José again?

Very sad. I think I would miss José if I had to give him up, but leaving Pepa is more difficult because she's more attractive. I feel empty when I'm not in drag. My breathing, heartbeat, metabolism, really my whole body functions differently. I'm going to confess something to you. When I'm in drag, I seldom pee because it's harder to do it in the street. So I've got used to holding it. The same thing happens when I fall asleep with my makeup on: I have different dreams, with more intensity, more color and feelings. My sense of humor and language are also different. As a man my humor is sharp and sarcastic. But when I'm Pepa there are certain words, like "fuck," "bitch," or "queer," that I would never say as a woman. It's not conscious really; I just don't do it.

Are there people who know you as both a man and a woman?

One is my sister. She knows that I'm a transvestite and has seen me in drag. At first, she almost had a heart attack, even though I had prepared her for the occasion. But little by little she got used to it. However, I notice that she still reacts differently to me depending on whether I'm in drag or not. When I'm a woman, she'll talk to me about emotional stuff, relationships, fashion. When I'm dressed as a man, we talk about things like money, finances, and even soccer. It's not on purpose—it just happens that way. It's the same with my butcher. When I go dressed as a woman he's very sweet and gives me samples. But as a man, he's colder and more distant, and never gives me anything. I'm the same person, but he cannot deal with José and Pepa in the same way.

What is it that you like most about transvestism?

I love to have two faces and be beautiful in one of them. It would never occur to me to have my penis removed because it's such a great source of pleasure. Really, I feel lucky for being able to have sensations that most people, out of fear, would never dare to have. There is nothing better than being able to make love to a man after he's done the same thing to you. This for me is like winning the lottery. There are thousands of men who would look gorgeous in drag but they'll never dare to make the leap. They are going to be toads all their lives when they could have been princesses, *excusez-moi,* queens.

There are people who would say that man and woman are made for each other and their sexual organs are complementary.

That's the worst sort of bullshit. Men report to me that sex with women is not that good. In the first place, women have different organs than men. They last longer, and sometimes never come. Men have to rub their clitoris to arouse them, sometimes it hurts, and sometimes they don't feel like it. Men usually aren't sure if they came or not because they're experts at faking orgasms. Female genitals, my clients tell me, are foreign territory and they don't know how they work. Men, on the other hand, feel tight when you're making love to them. When a woman starts lubricating, she sometimes becomes too loose. Some men tell me it gets worse after childbirth. With a transvestite however, you know when he's coming. You can also do it at the same time and you know what to touch because his body is the same as yours. Once you've both ejaculated, you can then relax and not have to worry about your partner having multiple orgasms, as is the case with women. Do you think it's really better with a woman?

What's the down side of it?

Discrimination, mockery, harassment, lack of understanding and, worst of all, the lack of large sizes in women's shoes.

A Few Succeed

Of course, some transvestites have realized their dream of becoming truly glamorous. Alma Stone, for one, met an Italian businessman who took her to Rome, where she now works for an exclusive clientele. With the money she is earning she plans to have a sex-change operation in Belgium. The following is a passage taken from a letter Alma sent to a friend in Costa Rica:

> I am really happy in Italy. Men here are very handsome and there's little harassment. It's totally different from Costa Rica where you're always being hassled by the police or by people on the street. Enrico took me to a first-class joint called "The Night Out" which only employs transvestites. I charge $500 for sex. Can you imagine how many Costa Rican dicks I would have to suck for that kind of money? Clients here really do treat you like a queen. Three weeks ago an entire team of soccer players came to the bar. They offered to pay $500 to the one who made them hard first. They all got undressed and their manager was chosen to be the judge. If you had been here you would have done it for free because they were all really good-looking. Gina was the one who won the prize since she dances and moves her tongue like a boa constrictor, which drove them crazy.

Doris Faye, another transvestite, now owns an upscale night club in Chicago. She has also been remarkably successful.

> I came to Chicago without any money at all. I used to clean houses and work as a waitress or a receptionist in cheap hotels. I was illegal and all the money I saved I sent to my family in Punta Arenas. One day I met this business executive who asked me out. In my bad English I told him that I was really a man and didn't want any hassles. He told me he knew and said that he wanted to get to know me. We had sex that same night. Next day, he sends me this beautiful ring. We dated for a couple weeks before he proposed to me. We finally got married by this gay pastor and I've been with him now for nine years. Mike gave me this nightclub to have fun with. I've

made money with it and we organize great drag shows. Our girls live like queens.

In another case, Gloria Day, a boy from San Pedro de Poás in Alajuela, became a famous jazz singer in New Orleans. His effeminate appearance and delicate features made him look stunning as a woman. He had been brought to the United States by a sailor whom he had met in San José. In a similar vein, Augusta now works as a model in Milan and has started to design her own line of clothes. Although she has no plans to return to Costa Rica, she continues to send money to her family in Cartago so that they might buy their own home.

Thus, as is attested to by these stories, there are cases in which transvestites' dreams of riches and fame come true, even if the latter only last as long as they can preserve their youthful appearance. For most, however, deep-seated societal discrimination ensures that they remain more toad than princess, with many retiring after a few years, if they have not already been killed by drugs, AIDS, gay bashers, or by their own hands through suicide.

Chapter 3

The Neighbors

Over the past ten years, a number of significant changes have taken place within San José's transvestite community. First, there has been something of a geographical shift. In the 1980s most transvestites lived and worked in an area known as El Libano (so called because of the presence in the neighborhood of a well-known movie theater catering to gay men). Most were poor, as were their clients, who were either working-class men employed in area stores, canteens, and markets, or rural laborers who traveled in and out of San José via the local bus station. However, since 1990 growing numbers of transvestites moved to a new locale, known as Clinica Biblica, in the city's southeast. This area is attractive to transvestites engaged in the sex trade for several reasons: not only is it quiet and close to downtown, but it is characterized by a more middle-class clientele.

As one might imagine, a number of factors were at work in inducing middle-class men to become involved in such numbers with the transvestites of Clinica Biblica. Transvestites themselves were at a loss when asked to account for the shift in client profile or why the "strip" had relocated at the time and in the manner that it did. Most referred to the increasingly tight housing market in Libano, leading many to look toward the city's southern and southeastern neighborhoods, where rented accommodation remained relatively cheap. Still, this does not explain the popularity of Clinica Biblica, located as it is between the Libano and downtown.

What we do know, however, is that the growing numbers of relatively wealthy clients have served to drive up the price paid for sex, while at the same inducing more and more transvestites, many of them young, beautiful, and middleclass, to become involved in the sex trade as well. Of course, this change in San José's sexual geography has not served the Libano district and the transvestites who continue to live there well. The bulk of the latter are older and retired from active involvement in the prostitution business, though they continue to suffer from its ill effects, including health problems, widespread substance abuse and, for many, grinding poverty in run-down boarding houses. As Laura put it, the "Libano has become a garbage dump and cemetery for transvestites."

THE LIBANO

When we first did our first series of interviews in 1990, most of San José's transvestite community was concentrated in the Libano district, with the majority living in the neighborhood's many cheap hotels, boarding houses, and brothels; very few lived with their families.

The Boarding Houses

In the 1980s, one of the most well-known boarding houses for transvestites was the Pension Romantica, a rambling old mansion with ten bedrooms. When I visited it in 1990, it was still in its prime. Each room was divided into two sections, and everyone shared the house's single bathroom and sink for washing clothes. Moreover, the house was seldom quiet. "Mayela Maria," screamed one transvestite, "where's the padding I lent you?" "I'm still using it," the other replied. "Can I keep it one more day?" "Fucking queen," the first one shouted, "when are you going to buy some yourself?"

For the most part, the bedroom walls are decorated with posters of naked men and Hollywood actresses, blown-up photos of the room's occupant in drag (usually in the pose of the starlet whose name she has taken as her own), along with assorted wigs and clothes hanging from nails driven into the plaster. As I glanced through an open doorway, a fat man in a wig greeted me. "Hey there, my name's Elizabeth Taylor," he said, holding up a large picture of the actress taken with her *Cat on a Hot Tin Roof* co-star Paul Newman. I did not have the heart to tell him, but I found he looked more like Don Francisco in drag than the famous actress with violet eyes. "The only thing he's got in common with Liz Taylor is his big ass," interrupted another transvestite from down the hall. The fat one ignored the insult, and invited me into her room. I looked around as I went in, and saw four black wigs, all of which were worn out and singed, along with a threadbare pink satin bedspread covering the bed. Some cheap nightgowns hanging in the closet were half hidden by an old sheet with a pattern of red roses. She took out one of the nightgowns. "Richard Burton gave this to me for our second wedding. I've only worn it once because of its deep sentimental value." The nightgown was made of blue velvet, with fake black pearls sewn in around the neck; some of the pearls were missing. According to Liz, Burton bought it himself for her at Fashion Palace, a clothing store in San José. However, her friend Penelope offered a different account of its origins. In her version, the nightie was made from a satin curtain which Liz had stolen from the Libano movie theater.

Pension Romantica, like most of the boarding houses inhabited by Libano's transvestite community, had a steel door to prevent unexpected visits by disgruntled clients or the police. To be let in, residents were required to identify themselves to those inside; otherwise, the door would not open. For this reason, transvestites' houses were known as "bunkers."

"Open the goddamn door, you deaf queen," I heard one transvestite shout from outside, angry at the slow response to her knocking. "Can you believe it," she said as she was let in, "I didn't get a single trick today. I walked up and down all day and didn't make a cent. At this rate I'll be poorer than a barefooted nun." "Well, barefooted you'll be if you don't pay the two thousand colones you owe me," replied the gatekeeper.

The Hotels

The typical establishment is characterized by a dirty curtain covering the door, through which one passes to a large room with red furniture (red being transvestites' favorite color) and pictures of men with oversized penises on the wall. Beyond this is the office where the hotel administrator works and sleeps. In it, one typically finds a mattress on the floor and a desk serving the dual function of clothes drawer and deposit for articles pawned by transvestites who need money for drugs (the administrator's second job is that of drug dealer).

I could hear a conversation going on as I pushed my way past the curtain into the first room, and upon poking my head into the office, I saw a skinny transvestite, dressed only in panties, speaking earnestly to the man behind the desk: "Look, this watch used to belong to Prince Philip, son of Juan Carlos of Spain. I bought it in Barcelona four years ago, and since I'm strapped for cash I have to sell it." To my eyes it looked like an ordinary Seiko. "The second hand has disappeared," she added, "but it still tells the hours." Liz, who was by my side, interrupted her: "The only thing this watch has in common with royalty is the fact that there's a queen trying to sell it. Penelope stole it from a john last night."

Beyond the office, there was a long hallway with bedrooms on either side. Interestingly, none of the rooms had doors; all had been removed and replaced with curtains. These, it seemed, proved useful at times when discreet entry and exit were required, for example when a transvestite wished to rifle through the valuables of a john who was in the middle of sex with someone else. Of course, there were those who would deny that any such thing takes place. "No!" exclaimed Penelope to one of her clients. "How can you even suggest that somebody stole your chain? Here you'll only find honest, hard-working prostitutes. You must have lost it yourself. We even pay our municipal taxes!" "Listen to me, you fucking whore," replied the john, "either you give me back my chain or I'll cut off your little shit-filled tits!" The transvestite thought about it for a moment, and then handed the chain over. "Oh yes, your chain! Here it is. I forgot that I found it on the floor a little while ago." The man grabbed it and made for the door, telling me as he passed, "If you're going to sleep with one of these faggots, leave everything you own at home." After he had left, Penelope told me who he was. "That brute owns a stall selling chayote near the Central Market."

In general, each bedroom contains nothing more than a bed, a couple of chairs, a small table for rolling joints or snorting coke, and a roll of toilet paper. The walls and sheets are usually dirty. "Here, we're both clean and ecologically friendly," explained Carla. "How's that?" I asked. "Because we ask the johns to help us try to conserve water, just like the best hotels, and we only wash the sheets once a month." In addition to sex, these rooms are also used for drug consumption by the transvestites and their friends. Given that it was the hotel manager who sold them the drugs in the first place, there is generally no problem in consuming them on the premises. Through one doorway, I saw three transvestites smoking crack. "Hey, do you want a pipe?" Rebecca asked me. "No, thanks," I answered.

Beyond the bedrooms is a kitchen. Like the entrance foyer, it is decorated with posters of men and rock stars, and contains a large, round table surrounded by four chairs, an electric stove, various pots and pans, and a locked chest of drawers used to keep pawned articles. An effeminate, jolly-looking man greeted me. "Hi there, my name's Tina Turner and I'm the one who does the cooking around here. Right now I'm in the middle of preparing a banana soufflé for the queens of this castle," she said seriously. "You know that they have very delicate stomachs and that they don't eat any salt at all because of their high cholesterol." I didn't ask to see the soufflé. The kitchen was dirty and disgusting, and while there I saw a number of cockroaches scurrying across the floor. The cook tried to reassure me: "If I serve you some food and you feel sick, don't worry. Their royal highnesses have already had some and they're still fine." "That's okay," I said. "I just ate lunch, so I'm not too hungry."

When not being used to prepare culinary delights, the kitchen is also a place where the transvestites come to consume cocaine, an activity that will be explored in greater detail in subsequent chapters.

Like the kitchen, the bathroom looked as though it had never been cleaned, with old toilets and even older plumbing. Above the stalls (again without doors) were two crumpled signs saying "Adam" and "Eve." However, everyone used "Eve" because "Adam" was backed up and not working. Those wishing to shower had to stand on top of the toilet and use a hose hanging down from the ceiling. "Darling, where can I piss?" asked a john as he left one of the rooms. "The men's washroom is being renovated, so you'll have to do your business in this bottle," Julia told him.

The Apartment Blocks

Meanwhile, other transvestites shared (and indeed in some cases continue to do so) apartments in the Libano with one or more of their colleagues. In a typical case, Marie Antoinette lived in a complex with approximately twenty units. Upstairs were three bedrooms (she shares the unit with two others), while on the main floor there was a kitchen, dining room, bathroom, and living room. The apartment was filled with old, worn-out furniture, and the walls were festooned with posters of favorite artists or movie stars. Johns came to the house as though it were any other brothel.

Upon entering the living room, one's eyes were immediately drawn to the large rug in the center of the room, originally red but now a mottled gray. Several candles, each dedicated to a saint from whom favors were sought, were burning in a corner, while the room's only table was covered with clippings from fashion magazines and old issues of *Extra*,[1] along with a little bowl filled with potpourri and someone's leftover breakfast. The rest of the room was no less messy, with wigs and a large, cracked mirror hanging from nails in the wall, clothes draped over every available chair, several books about witchcraft and the occult lying on the floor, a photo of Marie Antoinette's lover turned upside down ("because this was how I felt after he left me," as she put it), and finally a few bottles of perfume and aphrodisiac potion sitting on a window sill. "This one never fails," she assured me, pointing to one of the bottles. "I sprinkled some of it onto the food of a member of parliament I was seeing, and after that he couldn't get enough of me. He even sent me to Miami using money for his constituents. I just love corruption."

From time to time one will come across true luxury items in the apartment, say a Persian carpet or some fine porcelain, only to find them gone by the time of one's next visit, exchanged for cash at the local pawnshop. Generally, these items were all stolen from clients' homes. "This painting is an original César Valverde,"[2] Sonia Marta informed me. "I took it from a john while he was sleeping." She then pointed to a statue of David leaning against the wall. "Do you know where this one came from? Anita stole it from a priest! She just loves doing penance," added Sonia Martha with a smile. "She's a very Catholic nutcase."

Of course, life in an apartment block is not without its problems. When Marie Antoinette first moved into the complex, she was harassed by her neighbors, who would bang on the door, ring the buzzer and then run off, laugh in her face, and tell her that she had made a pact with the devil. This went on for quite some time, until finally Leticia advised her to buy several bottles of cheap, strong-smelling perfume from the Lucky Palace, a neighborhood department store, mix them all together, and then go around to each of her neighbors' apartments at midnight and spray the concoction all over their doors. Needless to say, the harassment largely ceased after this message was sent. Indeed, Marie Antoinette even went so far as to say that her relationship with her neighbors has become almost friendly:

> People around here treat me well. When I first came here I didn't know anyone but now I do. I've been here for two years now. My neighbors at the front are gay and they don't bother me. I say hi to the old woman over there, but the others I really can't stand, though everyone accepts us. "What's up?" I ask, and if they laugh I say, "Why is it that you laugh at me and not at your mother's cunt?"

The Migration

However, despite their long-standing presence in the Libano district, over the course of the 1980s many transvestites began the process of moving out of the neighborhood and into working-class districts mostly in the southern section of San José. Leticia remembers things being very difficult at the beginning:

> I'm now living in León XIII.[3] I love the life here and everybody knows me, though it was really bad initially. No one could stand me, though now I don't have any problems with the neighbors. From the beginning I felt I had two alternatives: either I split or to hell with the consequences and I stay up.

In somewhat similar fashion, Kristina moved into a house close to a church, and was faced with a priest who was extremely unhappy with her presence in the neighborhood.

> People told me that in his sermons the priest was calling me things like "sinner," "degenerate," and "fallen woman." One day I stopped him in the street and said, "Look, Pops, what's

your problem with transvestites?" The coward started backing away, saying how he loved us because we were all God's children. So I told him, "Look, you know that I know what you're up to at your pulpit. Why don't you worry about the children you like to fondle and leave me alone?"

Others moved into heterosexual brothels in the area. Patricia was one of the ones who did, even going so far as to share her living quarters with female prostitutes, all of whom were careful not to reveal her true identity to the johns. "But what happens when a client discovers that you're not really a woman?" I asked her. "It's very simple really. Some are so drunk that they can't tell the difference between man, woman, and beast in any case. Others get pissed off and leave. Most, however, stay put and pretend they didn't see anything."

Meanwhile, a few, Lucero among them, went so far as to set up gay brothels, often in the face of extreme hostility from nearby residents:

I can't say I'm too friendly with the neighbors around here. There's a lot of scandal mongering going on, and the kids call me "faggot," "queer," all sorts of stuff. I don't like it, and I try to avoid it as much as possible by keeping a low profile when I'm out in the street. Although we receive clients here, the truth is that it's often better to get tricks in the Biblica, since you know men with cars have got money. Also, the neighbors say how it sets such a bad example to have men coming in here.

In the early 1990s, one of the best-known establishments was that of Anna Karenina. Located next to a playing field, it housed no fewer than six transvestites at any given moment in time, all of whom were engaged in the sex trade on a more or less full-time basis. On the second floor of a two-story building, the brothel had five bedrooms, each occupied by a transvestite along with a lover or friend. On the main floor there was a heterosexual bar, and although there was occasionally friction between bar patrons and the transvestites, this was the exception rather than the rule. In short, each group had come to accept the other as simply part of the landscape.

As Anna Karenina put it, "I won't deny that it was difficult at the beginning, but now we've made our peace. We don't set foot in the bar and in return the drunks don't bother us upstairs." Even though this tacit understanding served for the most part to keep latent tensions in check, there were moments when conflict did erupt:

> One night someone shouted out that the building was on fire. I don't know if it was Angelica smoking at the back, but in any case we all ran out into the street, wearing nothing but bras and panties. The drunks from the bar started to hassle us and yell stuff like, "Come over here baby so I can spray you with my hose," you get the idea. So all of a sudden Agatha, who doesn't take any shit, went up to one of them and pulled down his pants. "This is no hose," she shouted, "this is a straw." After that they stopped screwing with us.

From the Suburbs to the Street

For the most part, San José's transvestites have abandoned the Libano cinema and the red light district that surrounds it, choosing instead to find housing in neighborhoods further away from the center of the city. However, this is not to say that everything has changed since the 1980s. Most significantly, their families continue to reject them, giving them little choice but to leave their own homes and move in with other transvestites.

As a growing number of middle- and upper-class adolescents are attracted to transvestism, more and more of them may be found prostituting themselves on the streets around the Clinica Biblica. Marilyn and Monica are typical of this trend. Marilyn grew up in Rohrmoser, and Monica's family lives in Escazú. Both of these neighborhoods are among San José's wealthiest suburbs. Moreover, both Marilyn and Monica continue to live with their parents, who have no idea that their sons dress up as women and are actively engaged in the sex trade. In the words of Marilyn,

> I'm from a good San José family. Nevertheless, I love dressing up as a woman and turning tricks on the street. I keep all of my clothes in one of the bunkers close to the Biblica. That's where

I go to change. One time I was picked up by no less than one of my dad's friends from work who's a doctor just like my dad. He's known me for years, but it didn't cross his mind that the voluptuous blonde who just got into his car was his colleague's little boy. He still comes over to my parents' place and he has no idea that I know his little secret.

Of course, by no means should one take the marked increase in the number of transvestites working the streets of San José as indicating that more are being born. Despite Esmeralda's observation that each weekend is characterized by the appearance of about five new transvestites in the district around Clinica Biblica, it is not a cloning machine that is producing them. Rather, the growth of the community is due to a number of factors, including greater middle-class acceptance of the phenomenon (both among the johns and the youths themselves) and, as will be shown below, the patent inability of the state to put a stop to the practice, whether it wishes to or not.

THE PAQUETEO REVOLUTION

While it is not particularly surprising that the Libano district would one day lose its status as the locus for San José's transvestite community, it is not at all clear why a geographic shift would in itself produce such a significant change in the transvestites' johns and lovers. In other words, why didn't the transvestites' old clients continue to seek out their services in the new red-light district? The answer is simple: because the new johns were wealthier and thus were able to offer the transvestites more money and a better standard of living. This, in turn, generates another question—where did the new clients come from?

In short, it appears that they were drawn from the relatively large number of men who were already coming to the quiet back streets of the Clinica Biblica neighborhood to obtain the sexual services of female prostitutes working there. At a certain point, however, the precise date of which none of the interview participants could remember with any certainty, the transvestites "took over" these streets, along with the johns who cruised them. In this way, the penetration of transvestites into the area cannot be seen merely as the replacement of one group of sex-trade workers by another. Rather, it encompassed nothing short of a sexual revolution. In traditional psychiatric terms, men who had formerly been exclusively heterosexual became bisexual overnight, as they stopped picking up women, opting for transvestite men instead.

How is this possible? Can sexual orientation truly be so elastic that heterosexual men can be "converted" to bisexuality in such a manner? As one might imagine, the answer is both yes and no. On one hand, it is clear that the transvestites' client base had to come from somewhere, and those who had been their johns in the Libano district had neither the money nor the means to travel across town to the new strip. For the most part, the johns were either day workers or unemployed. Meanwhile, as our interviews with the transvestites have shown, not only did the new clients from the Clinica Biblica area tend to be car owners (a strong indicator of middle- or high-class status in less developed countries), but they were generally employed in white-collar professions as well. It is in this sense that the clients were "new"; however, this is not to claim that their "conversion" was either immediate or entirely free of tension.

How so? When we attempt to determine the identity of those who pioneered the migration to the Clinica Biblica area, it soon becomes apparent that they were precisely those who were most adept at *paqueteo*, the process whereby a transvestite renders herself so feminine in appearance that she is able to "pass" for a woman. In this way, the Clinica Biblica area was initially appropriated by transvestites who looked as feminine as the female prostitutes who were already working there, opening a space into which others, less feminine in appearance, could follow.

Susy, for example, remembers the early years when "I would go to the Biblica by myself and I'd look like any of the other prostitutes there." According to her, at the beginning neither the johns nor the other sex-trade workers suspected that she was a man. Some of the clients would kick her out of their cars when they realized the truth. Nevertheless, little by little, "The johns started to get into it and after a few months some of the clients started to say that they liked doing it better with me than with the prostitutes. These guys recommended me to some of their friends, and they also asked if I knew any other transvestites they could meet." Susy went on: "At first I would only invite other *paqueteos*, but gradually I started to bring along others who were more masculine looking, until eventually the johns were into transvestites of all types."

It was the same with Zola. She never went back to the Libano once she had left, since she was so feminine that no one could tell she was a man simply by looking at her. However, she confessed that "A few years ago it was fairly difficult to get picked up by straight men around here [in the Clinica Biblica], but it's getting easier all the time." In her view, "Transvestites have become a fashionable commodity in the sex trade around here. Anyway, prostitutes weren't much competition since they were all pretty haggard and not too hot in bed."

In this way, one might argue that johns' sexual preferences and tastes underwent something of an evolutionary change, itself the product of an accident of geography. If one or two transvestites had not migrated to this area at the time and in the manner that they did, it is quite likely that the johns would have continued to see the same prostitutes they always had. At the beginning, one presumes that they were angry to find out that they were with men and not women. Nevertheless, they slowly began to enjoy what the transvestites offered, thereby increasing demand for their services. Soon, the area was completely taken over by transvestites, while the female sex-trade workers were forced to migrate elsewhere. Still, it must be borne in mind that this was only a partial "conversion" for most of the johns, since in other respects their behavior remained predominantly heterosexual.

Needless to say, this phenomenon warrants further investigation. However, in the context of the present work, it was not possible to interview a sufficiently large number of johns to develop a clear understanding of their conversion to bisexuality. Instead, the evidence at our disposal is largely circumstantial, consisting first of automobile makes and license plate numbers, which we used to identify the clients. These revealed that most of them came from either a middle- or upper-class background. Second, we have the testimony of the transvestites themselves, who assured us that most of their clients were married professionals. Those who used to work in the Libano district emphasized that these clients were markedly different from those who engaged their services in the old red-light district. Similarly, in our interviews with Clinica Biblica home-owners, it was made clear that the johns who were now picking up transvestites were the same ones who had previously been seen cruising for female sex-trade workers. Finally, one might argue that there is currently a new wave of displacement gathering force, whose locus is some of the city's straight bars. In short, as we will see later, a new generation of *paqueteo* transvestites, the majority of whom are Panamanian, have started to frequent locales that had previously been exclusively heterosexual. As our interviews with these individuals demonstrate, their ability to "trick" men into be-lieving that they are women has served to attract an entirely new population of johns to the particular pleasures of the transvestite sex trade, echoing the turn of events in the Clinica Biblica area in the process.

Chapter 4

The Battle for Clinica Biblica

THE DISTRICT

Few buildings in San José's central core are as imposing as the National Theatre. Situated in the midst of manicured gardens, marble statuary, and a broad, tourist-filled plaza, its poise and elegance stand in mute witness to "official" Costa Rican culture and values. Heading south from the Theatre, one is soon confronted with yet another icon of official culture: the Colegio Superior de Señoritas, where the daughters of the country's ruling elite have received a "proper" education for more than a century. However, even here the effects of unsustainably rapid urban growth are in evidence: stonework stained black by smoke and exhaust fumes; pavement that is uneven and pitted; and garbage accumulating in the street.

If one continues south from the college things get even worse. The streets become increasingly narrow, the stench of diesel exhaust hangs in the air, and dirty water drips from eaves troughs onto the pedestrians below. Although this has become an area of bustling commercial activity, many of the neighborhood's long-time residents refuse to abandon their homes in favor of some distant suburb. So they cling tenaciously on, ensconced within their modest bungalows, protected from the dangers outside by bars across their windows and steel grating on their doors.

The Clinica Biblica sits in the middle of this neighborhood. Built in 1929 by Protestant missionaries, it has become one of the city's best known—and most expensive—medical centers, with a multi-floor extension of concrete and glass serving as an appropriate testament to its financial success. This is further underscored by the countless pharmacies, walk-in clinics, and parking lots that have sprung up in the vicinity of the Biblica.

Until a few decades ago, this was one of San José's most distin-
guished neighborhoods. Now, when night falls, the recent arrivals
take over its streets. Dressed in short skirts or hot pants, with low
necklines and high heels, between sixty and one hundred transvestites may be found working the area between the National Theatre
and the Colegio Superior de Señoritas on any given night, mincing
and cat-calling as a procession of prospective johns drive slowly by.

THE TRANSVESTITES

Walking along these streets one night when a fine rain was falling,
I was faced with what can only be described as an exercise in con-
trasts: Miriam's elaborate blue sequin dress next to Corinthia's white
miniskirt; Aurora's coiffed hair, expensive perfume, and black scarf
alongside Veronica's nondescript dress and ponytail.

Generally, all of the transvestites working the streets of the Clinica Biblica do so in groups of three. The majority are Costa Ricans,
though there are some foreigners as well, mostly Panamanians who
have come to San José because of the city's reputation for being
somewhat more accepting of transvestism than is the case in their
own country. Corinthia is one such individual. She arrived in Costa
Rica four years ago, and generally finds that the working conditions
are much better here; according to her, being a transvestite in Panama requires either that one pretend to be a woman twenty-four
hours a day, or else that one be prepared to face more or less
constant harassment. Miriam, meanwhile, has another explanation
for the large number of Panamanian transvestites working in the
San José sex trade: quite simply, one must have white skin and blue
eyes to make money in Panama. In Costa Rica by contrast, the johns
like the Panamanians' exotic beauty and quick tongues.

It has been roughly nine years since the transvestites took over
the Clinica Biblica, abandoning in the process their former haunts
around the Libano cinema. While some continue to live in the old
neighborhood, most of the transvestites now working the strip have
their homes elsewhere in the city. Consider, for example, Pandora,
who owns her home in San Pedro (to the east of the downtown
core), or Miriam, who rents a flat in the Biblica, but spends her
afternoons at her mother's house in Desamparados (a city at the
southern edge of the capital).

There have also been changes in the transvestites' workplace. While the street continues to play a key role in providing the initial point of contact between john and transvestite, the sex itself takes place either in a car or in a motel room. Of course, many also continue to receive clients in their own homes. Still, this is not to say that all is well for the transvestites of the Clinica Biblica; at the minimum, they must contend with a work site that is also a battlefield.

Upon this battlefield, a number of well-defined forces are arrayed against them. In one corner are those who come to the neighborhood simply to attack or harass the transvestites working there. In another are local residents and home owners who have organized in a bid to rid the neighborhood of its nighttime denizens. And finally there is the police, upholders of law and order, and the transvestites' sworn enemy.

THE COLORIENTOS

Pepa Carrasco arrives at the strip after nightfall. She stops on a corner next to a greengrocer. Wearing a short black skirt with a jacket to match, her hair in a simple blunt cut, she holds an umbrella to shelter herself from the rain. Her makeup is discreet and understated, her perfume delicate and sexy. It's not a good night; there are few cars, and even fewer prospective johns. When a car finally does stop, she quickly realizes that it's not sex that the three young men inside are after. "Son of a bitch, faggot, whore, fucking queer!" they shout as they throw rotten eggs at her. Poor Pepa is forced to beat a hasty retreat, throwing a rock at the car as she flees. Her clothing, makeup, and perfume are all ruined, as are her night's prospects.

Monique, meanwhile, remembers being stopped by four men who asked her if she wanted a ride. Once on the outskirts of the city, near the Zurqui tunnel, the men raped her and then threw her onto the road. "Fucking whore, you don't deserve a penny, ugly faggot that you are," they shouted as they pushed her out. Monique had to hitch a ride on a banana truck to get back to San José.

As for Mimi, she was once assaulted by a group of students in the area around the Costa Rica High School. They shouted obscenities at her as they threw stones, one of which broke a tooth. Then, when she arrived at the Calderón Guardia Hospital, the staff refused to treat her. "Sorry sir, but I'm sure you've got AIDS and I don't want to go anywhere near your blood," she was told in the laboratory.

Anna Karenina recalls being splashed with urine after a man on a moped grabbed her purse. "Filthy dog, shit face, whore, heretic! Repent your sins and give yourself to God," he yelled as he drove away. Esmeralda remembers her early days on the street, when she didn't yet know that she should be wary of cars with tinted windows or driving at high speeds: "They yelled I don't know what as they drove by and threw a bottle at me. It hit me on the head and I needed five stitches to close the wound."

Of course, the greatest irony is that, despite the violence directed toward them, it is the transvestites themselves who are accused of being dangerous criminals who routinely carry rocks and knives. It is the same old story—blame the victim and in so doing avoid addressing the real issues at hand. In Costa Rica, there is a long tradition of such behavior toward Jews, who were accused of being communists; blacks, who were denied entry into many businesses and offices; Indians, who were deemed to be second-class citizens; and women, who were called "hysterical" for speaking out about male violence. In all cases, marginalization and persecution are justified though a twisted logic which transforms victims into the authors of their own misfortune.

Now the authorities are accusing a new minority of going about armed with dangerous weapons. But the question that remains un-answered is, who initiated this cycle of violence and who is respon-sible for perpetuating it? The answer is simple: those who hate transvestites. Yet they are not the only ones implicated in this regard; church and state must also shoulder part of the blame, given the extent to which they uphold a homophobic value system that pro-vides the climate necessary for gay bashing to continue unchecked within the population at large. A sermon that equates homosexuality with perversion and sinful behavior is doing little more than fanning the flames of hatred. "Society must be freed of such moral blights as homosexuality, prostitution, and transvestism," intones one priest being interviewed on television. Others speak loudly of the "corrup-tion, sin, and immorality" of gay men. Of course, by virtue of these venomous words the church has no need to dirty its own hands in pursuit of the goal of ridding the earth of homosexuality; others are induced to do so on its behalf. Of course, the parallels with the fascist era are obvious: although the church was not itself responsible for carrying out the Holocaust against the Jews, it provided ample moral cover for those who did. Within this context, the proviso that "we hate the sin but love the sinner" is, as Pepa puts it, "pure bullshit": "The Germans didn't distinguish between sin and sinner as they hauled the Jews off to the gas chambers."

Colorientos[1] is the name given to the men who come to the Clinica Biblica area to harass or, in some cases, attack any transvestites they may find there. "We call them *colorientos* because, as they're driving by yelling 'faggot' or some other insult, you can see their faces turning pink," explained Herman Loria, the coordinator of Priscilla, an ILPES program serving the neighborhood's transvestite community.

Generally, the *colorientos* arrive in the Biblica armed with rocks, plastic bags filled with excrement or urine, and even pellet guns. The pocked walls of local buildings, along with the scars on the bodies of area transvestites, provide ample testimony to the seriousness of the attackers' intent. Moreover, many *colorientos* will pose as johns to entice transvestites to their cars and, once they're close enough, the *colorientos* beat them.

"It's all a game to them. They see it as a way to let off some steam, assert their manhood, and express their homophobic tendencies. You could almost say it's a form a catharsis for them," suggested Loria.

In his opinion, society's traditional rejection of homosexuality is reinforced when a man is seen dressed up as a woman, and so taunts and insults are resorted to as ways of setting the person on the right path. "Perhaps if I insult you enough I'll be able to teach you that what you're doing is wrong. The message is simple: if you change your ways, I'll stop taunting you," he added.

Not surprisingly, the attacks draw their own response from the transvestites, who have taken to keeping rocks at the ready should they have the opportunity to heave one through the windshield of a passing *coloriento's* car.

JOHNS AND NEIGHBORS

Thus, the Biblica is not a particularly welcoming area for transvestites, who typically work there until the early morning hours. However, the precise time at which individual transvestites leave varies according to personal preference and the business prospects for the night. For example, Emperatrix typically goes home between one and two in the morning, while Corinthia and Miriam tend to stay on until two and three respectively. Finally, Pandora, who after almost two decades of work in the sex trade only goes out on Fridays and Saturdays, generally calls it a night at three o'clock, though she will occasionally stay out until six if conditions appear to warrant it.

Needless to say, the transvestites' presence in the area around the Clinica Biblica has served to attract hundreds of men who come to the area in search of sex. The noise generated by their vehicles, combined with the shouts of *colorientos* and the transvestites' equally vulgar replies, ensure that the transvestites' presence does not go unnoticed by those who live there. This noise is aggravated in turn by those who sit in their cars and leave their sound systems blaring, while the transvestites dance to the music on the sidewalk nearby. Finally, the sex trade itself is not a quiet activity, whether it is taking place on the street, or in the neighborhood's back alleys and vacant lots.

The residents, meanwhile, are forced to put up with this hullabaloo on a nightly basis, regardless of the fact that many moved to the area long before it became a commercial zone—in some cases thirty or forty years ago—and many see it as their only home, a home that has become increasingly unlivable in the wake of the transvestites' arrival.

"For the past nine years we've had to endure a blight that doesn't let us live in peace," remarked Olga, whose house—which she shares with her elderly parents—is situated two blocks away from the Clinica Biblica:

> I once had the misfortune of seeing oral sex in progress, one man masturbating another, while one finds condoms everywhere, urine and excrement on our doorstep. Then, after a certain hour in the evening, they start drinking liquor, fighting each other, using drugs. All these things have made our life unbearable. Their presence here brings with it all sorts of unwelcome visitors, like the kids who come here to throw stones and yell at them, while using the most foul language

imaginable. The circus starts at six p.m., and by ten it's unbearable. Paydays and weekends are the worst. Right up until Sunday. . . . It's all the time really. Then, if we dare to look out the window, they consider it a mortal sin. If they see us out on the sidewalk, they yell at us. If they don't see us, they yell at us anyway. We just can't win.

Of course, it is not merely the behavior of the transvestites and their clients that bothers the residents; it is also the fact that their presence has pushed property values downward. "No one wants to rent, no one wants to buy our houses," complained Priscilla, a local homeowner.

One night at three in the morning I heard the window rattle. I thought at first it was a burglar trying to break in. When I pulled back the curtain to take a look, what did I see but somebody pushing his big black penis into a woman out there. "My God," I screamed, "what is this?" Then I heard a transvestite yelling back at me, "Don't sweat it, lady, you know exactly what's going on." I was so angry that I shouted back, "Why don't you have some respect for us? Some of us are older women and we don't want to have to see this sort of filthy behavior going on right outside of our own homes." But he couldn't care less. He just shouted, "Well then, why don't you tell this guy to have some respect for me and be more careful where he's sticking his dick."

In another case, Lupita remembers her eight-year-old son coming up to her one day and asking her what "powder" meant. "Well, my dear, powder is a sort of fine white dust that women use for make-up," she told him. "So if that's all it is, why is the transvestite down the street selling it in a little bag for five thousand colones?" Lupita didn't quite know what to say, so she just told him that "Some types of powder are more expensive than others."

Mario, also a member of the residents' association, recalls several occasions when transvestites would engage in intercourse on the street outside his home. "Three weeks ago I saw a transvestite get into a car and start to have sex. Not only do they not let us sleep in peace, but every time that guy came close to coming, he would hit the car horn. I couldn't stand it any more, so I ran outside and yelled, 'Why the hell are you blowing that car horn at me? You degenerate!' And then from the car the transvestite yells back at me, 'Go back to sleep, you pervert. What are you doing spying on me anyway?'" Soledad, another long-time resident of the neighborhood, had a similar experience. One night she discovered a transvestite passionately kissing a client right outside her door. "Miss, would you mind awfully kissing somewhere else?" she asked politely. "Forget it, you old bag! Can't you see how hard it is for this old guy to get it up? If we move, he'll lose it," was the transvestite's answer.

THE ASSOCIATION

The residents have tried to address these problems through various means, going both to the police and to the courts. They have also appealed to the office of the governor of San José, who committed himself about four years previously to "clean up" the capital, cracking down on brothels, unlicensed drinking establishments, and so forth. He has also gone before the Constitutional Court to obtain special powers to protect the interests of the Biblica residents, as well as approaching the public ombudsman and community organizations that work with transvestites.

Four years ago the residents decided to form an organization called the Neighbors' Association of Clinica Biblica, whose principal purpose was to lobby public bodies such as the National Assembly, requesting for example that the laws governing prostitution be changed to increase the penalties for those caught.

In the final analysis, the group sees only one solution for the problem at hand: the complete removal of all transvestites from the area around the Clinica Biblica. Focusing their efforts on this single objective, they have gone on the warpath, while a range of outside groups have positioned themselves in either one camp or the other.

For Loria, an expert in the field currently working with ILPES, Costa Rican democracy continues to be characterized by a sizeable gap between rhetoric and reality. That is to say, one must not forget that transvestites enjoy the same protections under the constitution as anyone else, and thus one cannot simply take away their right to free movement as a matter of course. Of course, this is not to say that

Loria is unaware of the problems facing Clinica Biblica residents, and from this point of view their frustration is understandable, a point which many transvestites would concede as well.

As he put it, "One can't say that it's not an awkward situation. The neighbors don't want them, but the transvestites have every right to be there and in fact are insisting that they don't want to move anywhere else."

Three years ago an accord was reached whereby the transvestites agreed to avoid residential streets and work only in the commercial sector, but the near-constant arrival of new transvestites on the scene has made incursions into residential areas more or less inevitable.

THE GOVERNOR

Jorge Vargas was the governor of San José and the main force behind the capital's cleanup campaign, for which he received both praise and opprobrium in roughly equal measure. Subscribing to the motto "first in place, first in right," he argued that the residents' complaints must be taken seriously because they were already living in the area before the transvestites' arrival.

Far from taking a moral stance on the issue (i.e., in terms of the sexual orientation or activities of the transvestites), Vargas took refuge in his mandate to justify his actions. In short, because it was his duty to maintain order in the capital, he claimed that he had no choice but to clamp down on those whose nighttime activities disturb the peace of a community that has been in place for years. As he put it, "I have to intervene in order to avoid conflict on an even larger scale."

According to Vargas, he organized meetings which have brought together the parties to the conflict, as well as tabling several possible compromises. Well aware that he could not legally force the transvestites to restrict their activities to a particular geographical area, and prevented from creating a "tolerance zone" within the Biblica, Vargas, together with the head of the police force and the public ombudsman, advocated the relocation of the transvestites to a commercial sector of the city where they could carry out their activities without hindrance.

At one time the area around González Viquez Square was mooted as a possible relocation site, but the proximity of the Costa Rica High School, with its large population of young students and potentially disapproving teachers, quickly served to make this location politically impracticable. The other option considered was the park in front of the former Pacific Electric Railway Station, an area relatively close to Clinica Biblica, but almost completely devoid of any private residences.

THE PUBLIC OMBUDSMAN

This last alternative was preferred by the public ombudsman who had been called in to mediate in the dispute, and with whom the transvestites had already lodged three complaints in the past.

Adjunct ombudsman Rolando Vega, who has followed the conflict closely, is quite emphatic in his assertion that while the residents should be free to enjoy their rights, they cannot expect to do so at the expense of the rights of others. In this way, any solution to the conflict must take adequate account of two distinct sets of rights: those of the transvestites to free movement, which could very well be violated should a "compromise" be unilaterally imposed upon them, and those of the residents to live in peace, which, under present circumstances, are being violated on a daily basis.

Thus, according to Vega, "The challenge facing us right now is how to arrive at a solution that does not trample on either party's rights. The transvestites have to understand that, although they themselves have rights, their presence does generate significant problems for the neighbors. It is for this reason that I see relocation as the most reasonable way of resolving this issue."

Needless to say, relocation remains a contentious issue. The transvestites are far from willing to give up a place of work that sustains them economically, and that they have spent years developing. Still, the authorities insist that transfer of the red-light district to a nonresidential area is the only workable way of resolving the dispute.

There is a widespread sense among the parties involved that the conflict could easily escalate into something considerably more serious. Certainly, the residents have not lost any of their resolve to rid Clinica Biblica of its transvestite population. At one time, soon after the founding of the Neighbors' Association, members initiated a campaign in which they wrote down the license plate numbers of cars coming into the area in search of transvestites. Once they had identified the cars' owners, they would call to tell them that they were aware of their activities, and were prepared to identify them publicly.

Now, the residents are beginning to contemplate other, more aggressive tactics. "For my part I wouldn't resort to violence, but there are many who've offered to help us," remarked one neighbor. Some of the residents have said that a confrontation is inevitable, and that they are thinking about "getting a gun and shooting one of these sons of bitches. People around here are tired of waiting for solutions that never come. It's been suggested that we should hire some vigilantes, and we've even been offered shock troops, but we don't want to hurt anyone. But, if we get desperate enough, we just might turn to the Free Costa Rica Movement."[2]

THE POLICE

If there is one point on which both transvestites and residents agree, albeit for different reasons, it is that no one appears to want police intervention in the dispute.

The residents say that they are disappointed with the latter's seeming inability to stop the transvestites from frequenting the area, which they believe is because the police do not take the problem seriously. The neighbors also recognize that many police officers, far from working toward a solution to the problem, are merely interested in attacking the transvestites to rob them or "even take advantage of them sexually." As for the transvestites themselves, their reason for being distrustful is far more simple: the police persecute transvestites as no one else does.

This view appears to be borne out by the fact that, until quite recently, police officers were given free rein to harass transvestites at will, something that local advocacy groups believe was directly related to the governor's cleanup campaign, to the extent that front-line officers were being ordered to bring under control the delinquency that was thought to derive from the transvestites' presence in the area. Thus, it was common for transvestites to be detained in a police station holding cell for hours on end, without any explanation whatsoever from the authorities.

Transvestites' generally low level of education ensured that, even though they theoretically enjoyed the same constitutional rights as any other Costa Rican citizens, the majority had no means of accessing the tools and resources needed to assert these rights. As Loria put it, in some cases "they don't even think they're worthy of human rights."

However, the creation of the Constitutional Court (*Sala Cuarta*) changed all this. Since its inception, the transvestites have gone before it three times with complaints, alleging gross violations of their basic human rights. While their charges were deemed groundless in the two of the cases, the presiding magistrates found in favor of the transvestites in the final one.

This case involved a habeas corpus complaint against members of San José's third and fifth precincts, lodged by four transvestites who were arbitrarily arrested in May 1997 by officers of the motorcycle unit. Despite handing over their identification papers (which were in order), the police officers proceeded to arrest them, though not before relieving them of their money. In addition, according to the complainants, not only did these officers fail to comply with normal arrest procedures, but the transvestites were subjected to various indignities along the way.

THE CONSTITUTIONAL COURT

Following their release, the transvestites decided to initiate proceedings against the officers in Costa Rica's Constitutional Court, alleging violations under the terms of Articles 22 and 39 of the Political Constitution, and Articles 7 and 8 of the American Human Rights Convention, which guarantee the right of free movement to all citizens. Furthermore, in relation to the Political Constitution in particular, it guarantees every Costa Rican freedom from arbitrary arrest and detention, along with the right to unrestricted movement and abode anywhere in the country.

In their ruling, the magistrates found in favor of the transvestites, arguing that the police had acted improperly in arresting the complainants without due cause. In the wake of this decision by Costa

Rica's highest court, police officers were only able to proceed against transvestites in cases where they had reasonable grounds to believe that a crime had been committed (i.e., they had received a complaint) and, should an arrest be warranted, it could only be undertaken in relation to the particular crime that the individual in question was suspected of committing. Since this ruling police treatment of transvestites has improved considerably, and is now thought to differ little from that which is meted out to other segments of the population. Still, despite the change, there can be little doubt that the label "persecutor" remains fixed in the minds of many transvestites.

Indeed, there are some who would argue that the relationship between transvestites and police continues to be a thoroughly violent one, with officers showing scant respect for individuals whom they see as undermining traditional values by dressing up as women and prostituting themselves. In Loria's estimation, "It would seem the police think that they're doing the transvestites enough of a favor by letting them live, so they certainly shouldn't expect the right to speak out."

The transvestites, meanwhile, see policemen as authority figures par excellence, who have always endeavored to make their lives miserable. In their minds, the police are typically equated with arrest, humiliation, detention, and loss of money.

For a typical example of this relationship, one need only consider the countless nights in the past when a group of police officers would suddenly appear in the Clinica Biblica district, and order all the transvestites present to leave the area or face arrest. Any hint of resistance would be met with beatings, baton charges, and the paddy wagon.

Once inside the paddy wagon—the *"cajón"* in local parlance—the transvestites would be thrown around its hard interior as the driver deliberately braked and accelerated in quick succession. Eventually they would arrive at the precinct headquarters where, if they were lucky, a ticket would be filled out. However, to the extent that arresting officers have become fearful that those detained may later try to launch appeals against them, they often now refrain from registering the arrest in the first place, thereby hoping to preempt any such action.

Once in the cell block, again if they were lucky, they would spend a few hours there before being released. If luck were not on their side, they would be ordered to strip down and parade in front of everyone, under threat of being beaten. As they did so, they would be taunted and their bodies made fun of, all of which was humiliating in the extreme. Then, finally, they would be released at dawn, with a night's work ruined.

Chapter 5

Priscilla and Prevention

Generally speaking, few homosexual populations are more open about their sexual orientation than gay transvestites, who are characterized by extremely high indices of socialization. As one might imagine, this is because transvestism and effeminacy together serve to make them among the most obviously gay men of all Costa Rica. As Anna Karenina recounts, whenever she is not dressed as a woman, she is always being recognized as a gay man:

> I'm so queer that even when I'm dressed in men's clothes and acting all macho, I don't fool anyone. One day I went out to buy some vegetables and I was putting on this show of being really gruff and aggressive, talking like a man and so on. But, as I was heading out the door, the clerk said to me, "Hey baby, don't you want to see the yucca I've got for you?"

Kristina has had similar experiences: "Who am I going fool when I'm wearing pants if I've got a pair of tits as well?" Others meanwhile have had to contend with problems of a somewhat different sort. Ana Louisa recalls the day that she dressed as a man to go to her nephew's first communion. She was quite happy with herself because she thought she had tricked all those in attendance. Indeed, so well did she play the part of the macho that she decided to relieve herself in the men's washroom. However, as she was standing at a urinal, she heard someone say, "What's the dyke pissing in here for?"

In this way, it is not particularly surprising that transvestites are widely recognized as gay, whether they are dressed as women or not. Consider for example the fact that 73 percent of transvestites'

parents know their child's sexual orientation, compared to 24 percent in the case of other gay men. This finding is further borne out
when one compares the rates for particular family members: among
mothers, the rate is 100 percent for transvestites and 52 percent for
other gay men, while among brothers it is 95 percent and 44 percent
respectively (see Table 5.1).

Given the fact that such a large proportion of transvestites' families are aware that their sons are gay, and that the great majority of
these are loathe to accept it, large numbers of young transvestites
end up living on their own or with friends, with only 14 percent of
transvestites continuing to live with their parents. Indeed, young
transvestites are more likely to be living with their friends (most of
whom are also homosexual) than any other subpopulation of the
gay community (Table 5.1).

TABLE 5.1. People with Whom One Normally Shares One's Place of Residence
(Percent)

Variable		Gay	Transvestite sex-trade workers
	(N)	(162)	(22)
	Total	100	100
Who do you live with most of the time?			
Alone		17.3	31.8
Parents or family		54.9	13.6
Wife/female partner		—	—
Male partner		11.1	9.1
Friends		13.6	45.5
Others		3.1	—
Persons with whom you live occasionally . . .			
Alone		4.9	—
Parents or family		10.5	4.5
Wife/female partner		—	—
Male partner		8.0	—
Friends		13.6	40.9
Don't live with others		61.7	54.5
Others		1.2	—

Source: Jacobo Schifter and Johnny Madrigal, *Hombres que Aman Hombres,*
San José, Costa Rica, ILEP-SIDA, 1992.

LACK OF SUPPORT AMONG TRANSVESTITES

Nevertheless, transvestites are less likely to seek the support of others when they themselves have problems. When they were asked whether or not they went to other transvestites for help, 45 percent said that they would not do so, while only 18 percent indicated that they always sought the help of others. In the case of gay men, only 10 percent said that they never went to their friends for support (see Table 5.2).

TABLE 5.2. General Sources of Help, Support, or Advice (Percent)

Variable		Gay	Transvestite sex-trade workers
	(N)	(162)	(22)
	Total	100	100
Friends			
Always		29.0	18.2
Very often		20.4	4.5
Sometimes		31.5	22.7
Rarely		8.6	9.4
Never		10.5	45.5
Gay organizations			
Always		1.9	0.0
Very often		1.2	4.5
Sometimes		5.6	4.5
Rarely		8.0	9.1
Never		79.6	81.8
Don't know/no response		3.7	0.0
Nongay organizations			
Always		1.2	4.5
Very often		0.6	0.0
Sometimes		4.3	0.0
Rarely		9.3	4.5
Never		80.9	90.9
Don't know/no response		3.7	0.0

Source: Jacobo Schifter and Johnny Madrigal, *Hombres que Aman Hombres,* San José, Costa Rica, ILEP-SIDA, 1992.

Thus, despite the intense socialization evident among transvestites, these findings suggest that they tend to view their colleagues as potential competitors (e.g., for clients), and thus not entirely trustworthy.

Transvestites are also more likely than other gays to agree with such statements as "promiscuity leads to AIDS" (41 percent of transvestites strongly agreed with this position, compared to only 14 percent of other gays); "you can't trust people who are homosexual" (64 percent of transvestites were somewhat in agreement with this statement, against 31 percent of other gay men); "AIDS is a form of divine retribution" (50 percent were in strong agreement, compared to only 9 percent of other gays); and "there is no such thing as a stable relationship because homosexuals are unfaithful" (64 percent of transvestites agreed strongly with this assertion, in contrast with 23 percent of other gay men).

In similar fashion, when they were asked what they thought of other transvestites, the responses were often highly negative:

> Here they're all bad, people don't respect each other. But if someone's going to yell at me, I'm going to yell right back at them. (Patricia)

> There's lots of scheming and hypocrisy. If something bad happens to you, they'll say "Oh, you poor dear" to your face, but it's all a front. In this environment no one trusts anyone else and although people used to try to screw me around, now I know how it works and so I defend myself. (Marlene)

> No one's worse than the sons of bitches around here. I hate them all, they're just a bunch of disgusting pigs. (Marilyn)

Given the passages quoted above, it should come as no surprise that venomous attacks upon others' self-esteem are common within the transvestite community. Just as society teaches its members to hate transvestism, so are transvestites taught to hate one another and themselves. Lucretia, for one, believes that common ground can never be found because "Everybody hates each other: either they're stealing from each other, or they're talking behind their back, or they're sleeping around with their boyfriends. No one is anyone else's friend." Rosa has tried in the past to organize the transvestites for self-help purposes, but, as she put it, "Before you knew it the envy was starting up, and then the quarreling, the venom, the messing up of other people's plans. . . . " Adriana, meanwhile, would argue that transvestites have learned too well the lessons that society has tried to teach them: "We're our own worst enemies. We show each other less compassion than anyone else."

There is evidence of this venom everywhere. Pepa is known as the Rottweiler because this is what she is said to look like when she dresses in drag. Lola's nickname is Queen Mother because of her age. Penelope, meanwhile, is called Price-Cutter because of the low rates she charges her clients. Finally, Nidia is known as Ms. STD, because she suffers from syphilis and gonorrhea.

However, name-calling is not the only tactic used to put down others. Transvestites have also been known to steal from one another, spread false rumors or inform on others, seduce others' clients and lovers, and even in some cases kill one another. Pepa, for example, loves to submit anonymous complaints about colleagues to the police. Mirna remembers telling Sonia that Lulu stole 5,000 colones from her, even though she knew this was not the case. In another instance, Antonieta recalls breaking one of Rosita's teeth, "because she wouldn't give back a pair of shoes I had lent her." Meanwhile, Miriam once threw acid in Flor's face because "the little shit thought she was so beautiful." As for Enriqueta, she says that she never goes to the Biblica area: "Since I can pass for a woman, all of those dog-faced transvestites working there hate me."

Indeed, Tachita describes the transvestite community as one that is full of petty jealousies and intrigue: "The only reason we get together is to fight." This perspective is confirmed by Corinthia, who reports that relations among transvestites are not good, and that in some cases individuals will even resort to physical violence. Not without some bitterness, Herman Loria describes the situation thus:

> Those who are most attractive or most intelligent are criticized and ostracized because they get the best johns, and sometimes they'll even be attacked, since the feeling is, "If you're pretty I can cut your face to make you ugly." Meanwhile, those who are ugly are treated poorly as well.

INTERNAL DIVISIONS

Until fairly recently, much of the dissension within the transvestite community could be traced to intergenerational differences, with newly arrived individuals required to pass a series of tests (and suffer a few blows) before being accepted as full-fledged community members.

On the street, one encounters transvestites of all ages, ranging from sixteen- or seventeen-year-old adolescents to forty-year-olds who are burning out, and know it. As Valentina put it, "If I was a john there's no way I'd pick up a forty-year-old transvestite who's all worn out and decrepit, when there are young, virile ones about." At twenty-seven, she says that she tries to keep herself looking good, but is concerned by the small size of the Costa Rican market: "The clientele here is small, and so there are twenty transvestites on the street for every five johns."

In an example of this intergenerational tension, one night a group of transvestites from the Clinica Biblica area descended upon another group of younger transvestites who were congregating in another neighborhood. The reason? The older transvestites accused the younger ones of attracting johns by charging lower prices, and that this was unfair competition. As they pulled out their knives, one of the older ones snarled, "You starving bitches are turning tricks for three hundred pesos. If you want to stay alive, you better get the fuck out of here." On other occasions, the attacks have been directed toward foreigners.

However, things have improved in recent years, and today intergenerational conflicts are relatively rare. In particular, those who have just arrived on the scene tend to be quite cautious in their dealings with others until they are accepted by the group. According to Tachita, "The street is a tough school and when a new one shows up we have to teach her how to defend herself. Many of them are very innocent and they have to learn that life's not all roses."

Still, at the same time that age-related conflict diminishes, nationality-based tension increases. In the words of Azulita, "The main problem facing Costa Ricans is competition from other Central Americans and people from the Dominican Republic. That's the last thing we need, having a huge bunch of Nicaraguan and Panamanian refugees who come here to steal our money and our johns. The government should really stop letting these foreign whores into the country."

These feelings are exacerbated by a series of tensions related to turf and geography. "Transvestites working the Biblica district are high-class," asserted Leticia, "so the last thing we want up here are those slack-jawed whores from the Libano. They're so dirty and ugly that any john who sees them would never want to come back here again."

Finally, there is little solidarity between male transvestites and female sex-trade workers, with numerous conflicts arising over the years. In short, the transvestites insist that the women must stay away from "their" streets. "The hookers have got all of San José," pointed out Penelope, "so there's no reason why they should want to come here." The female sex-trade workers, for their part, resent the competition from the men, all the more so because some of the latter have better bodies than they themselves.

Nevertheless, if many transvestites feel contempt for others within their community, many of them have even less respect for other gays and lesbians. In particular, some will never forgive gay men for their masculine demeanor. Quite simply, they assume that every gay man has the potential to be a transvestite, but refuses to acknowledge this.

"Don't you think it pisses us off when we aren't let into a gay bar just because the owner is a piece of shit who doesn't want anyone in there who's dressed in drag?" asked Lucy.

A majority of gay men, despite being attracted to individuals of the same sex, have no desire to become women themselves. For this reason, many of them feel that transvestites have no place in their community. According to one gay-bar owner, "I don't let transvestites in because they're a terrible bunch, drunk all the time, addicted to coke and, on top of that, crooks and prostitutes. My clients like the masculine look and not these disgusting things dressed up as women who look like extras from some horror movie."

LACK OF SUPPORT FROM LOVERS

Of course, exacerbating these problems is the negative attitude of the transvestites' lovers, which may contribute in turn to the difficulty many transvestites experience in sustaining constructive relationships with their colleagues. This, in turn, is reinforced by transvestites' tendency only to socialize with other couples. Finally, it must be noted as well that the transvestites do not generally perceive their lovers as homosexual, which means that this source of support is not categorized as gay.

As will be emphasized in subsequent chapters, the transvestites' lovers tend to have certain characteristics in common. Most have previously been engaged in relationships with other transvestites, leaving a legacy of bitterness and jealousy. It is interesting to note in this regard that the bulk of the lovers' animosity is not directed toward the johns, but rather against other *cacheros* (men who have sex with men for money or lack of women, but are not considered homosexual) and the transvestites themselves. In this way, a circle of envy is created whereby lovers are jealous of other lovers, while the transvestites are jealous of all the other transvestites whom they fear may try to steal away "their" men.

José, for one, said that he keeps away from other transvestites because "there's always something going on between them. Most of them live for the chance to tell stories about other people or break up couples who are perfectly happy with each other. It makes me want to go out there and give them a good thrashing."

Meanwhile, Louis indicated that he does not generally go to the Biblica because Sylvia, his partner, becomes jealous when other transvestites look at him. In a similar fashion, Cynthia's lover Delio gets angry whenever he sees her talking with other *cacheros*, just as she does not like it when she catches him speaking with other transvestites. Moses reported that Miriam is jealous of him because "I tend to be very friendly with the other transvestites."

HOMOPHOBIA AND AIDS

As one might imagine, internalized homophobia plays an important role in explaining these feelings of jealousy and insecurity, as well as accounting for the tendency of many within the transvestite community not to take steps to minimize the chance of HIV infection. In short, individuals who are less accepting of their homosexuality often do not see themselves as part of a high-risk population, do not seek the support of others in the gay community, and may very well take ill-advised risks as a way of coping with the sexual identity issues they are facing.

OFF TO MIAMI?

"Don't push, ladies. There's room for everyone on LACSA, Costa Rica's national airline. Remember that we love our customers, especially those who are young and beautiful," announced a boy dressed as a flight attendant. "Please have your passports and U.S. visa in hand," he asked. The line is long and the girls are impatient. "You're only taking the one bag?" asked Sonia of Lulu. "I'm going to be buying all sorts of stuff in Dadeland and I don't want to bring so many clothes that they confiscate my luggage," she answered. Behind them in the line, Enriqueta and Agatha were engaged in a discussion that is best reproduced in its entirety:

> *Where do you plan on staying in Miami?*

> Definitely the Hilton, since I just hate second-rate hotels. How about yourself?

> *Oh, I'm staying at the Marriott. I've got a suite there. Are you going to go the beach at all?*

> You know very well that I'm just going to shop. Anyway, the sun dries out my skin and gives me wrinkles.

> *Really, I think you're not going to the beach because you don't want anyone to see the cellulite on your butt.*

> Cellulite, me? Never! My ass is as hard as rock.

> *Lunar rock, you mean—full of holes.*

> If my butt's lunar rock, I would say yours is probably a black hole.

Of course, the youths who are pretending to be heading off to Miami are not really boarding a LACSA flight, but rather an old, dilapidated bus known as Priscilla, a name inspired by a movie about a group of Australian transvestites who decide to travel across their country by bus. Despite its run-down appearance, the vehicle serves as a "plane" that takes its "passengers" (a group of transvestites) on a journey through the outskirts of San José. Meanwhile, the "flight attendant," who also acts as bus driver, works with ILPES. In this way, Priscilla is a novel AIDS-prevention initiative serving the transvestite community.

"Girls, please put on your seat belts because we're about to take off," enjoins the coordinator, "and please pay attention to the safety instructions."

> Although we are unlikely to encounter any problems during our flight, we have to have a condom ready at all times. Since we're flying with so many erections on board, there may be some turbulence. We must always be ready with our rubbers in hand. Many passengers have died in the past because they were caught by an air pocket without their condoms on. Also, please remember that we will be flying over water, so don't forget to blow up your life vest. Just cover the open end with your mouth, and start blowing. And don't fake it, ladies, because I know you're all experts.

"Why the use of aeronautical jargon in an AIDS-prevention initiative?" I asked Herman Loria, the project's coordinator. "Because it's a fun and nonthreatening way to bring together a group who work on the street and don't have any other places to get together. Also, the transvestites often find it difficult to get motivated about this sort of issue, and the bus gives them a chance to see something different and breathe some fresh air." He went on to say,

> The project tries to use fantasy in a way that transvestites are already familiar with, presenting a sort of "show" that also communicates a message about prevention. Not only do we talk about the importance of always using a condom, but we encourage them to seek help for their substance abuse as well. Finally, we're also trying to get them to organize a union, as a way of counterbalancing some of the pressure they're facing from johns and lovers. Moreover, it would give them a way of reaching some sort of consensus on the rates they charge, and

condom use could be made nonnegotiable. Also, we're trying to promote the creation of microenterprises, like putting on drag shows for fancy clubs and what not. This way they would have some alternatives to the sex trade.

As Loria proceeded to tell me about the project, the transvestites continued to entertain themselves with the airplane motif. "Mayela, would you mind awfully asking the steward for his pen so that I can fill out my landing card?" asked Julia. "Right now I've got it in my mouth, in case you haven't noticed," the other one replied.

Thus, ILPES has sought to devise an initiative that builds upon transvestites' innate sense of humor and sarcasm as ways of disseminating AIDS-related information, while at the same time serving to counteract the rivalries and distrust that have proved so destructive in the past. Opening up new spaces and possibilities for the transvestites is another objective, and involves attempts to find alternative ways for them to make a living. However, because of the problems discussed in previous chapters, this has not proved particularly easy or straightforward.

Nevertheless, one may point to particular bases for solidarity. One such basis is the police harassment suffered in common by transvestites, female sex-trade workers, johns, gays, and lesbians. In short, this persecution could very easily serve as a vehicle to empower these groups and induce them to undertake concerted action.

Other common ground exists in the advocacy and support organizations that have been established over the years. ILPES, for example, has organized workshops where the participants learn how their dislike and distrust for one another plays into the hands of their common enemies. Furthermore, recent legal victories against arbitrary arrest and detention have benefited everyone to some degree, to the extent that the police show greater care in their actions against minority groups.

The creation of antitransvestite organizations such as the Neighbors' Association of Clinica Biblica has given the transvestites another reason to organize themselves. The Neighbors' Association is the first of its kind in the country, and its explicit aim is to reverse the gains made by transvestites in the courts. Although the resi-

dents' prime concern at the moment is simply to drive the transvestites out of the Biblica area, one cannot assume that they will stop
here. Even more worrisome, is the possibility that other conservative groups will use the antitransvestite movement as a front as they
endeavor to attack the rights of gays in general, as has occurred in
recent years in the United States.

Chapter 6

The Business of Prostitution

In the era when most of San José's transvestites lived and worked in the area around the Libano cinema, it was clear that the vast majority of them hailed from very modest backgrounds. That is to say, their families were generally rural or urban poor people, and most had suffered extreme economic hardships in the past. It was highly uncommon to encounter individuals with middle- or upper-class family backgrounds.

Katrina, for example, lost her mother when she was very young, and was raised as a foster child by a wealthy family in Alajuela:

> I'm here because my mother died when I was eight and we suffered many hardships as children, me and my brothers. I went first to live with a family with money in Naranjo, the [. . .], and then afterwards I got to know the [. . .] in Sarchi and they raised me until I was fourteen. . . . I suffered a lot when I was young. They all abused me. For a few beans they thought they could use me all day. So finally I decided that I was better off selling my body for something a little more than a full stomach and a roof over my head.

Meanwhile, Gina, also from a very humble background, used to work in a factory but found that the money she made there was not enough to sustain her:

> I'm thirty years old, and am from Limón. Before coming here, I got a job in a factory after my eighteenth birthday. However, I've since got involved in prostitution. . . . At the factory, they worked us like slaves. I would only get half an hour for lunch

and they paid us a shit wage. And, on top of that, you had to sleep with the foremen. Several friends of mine, so as not to lose their jobs, had sex with them. One of them was famous for having raped a dozen of the workers. When this one found out that I was a transvestite, I was called into his office and ordered to undress so that he could check it out for himself. I told him to fuck his mother and I quit.

Antonieta was also forced into prostitution for financial reasons. She already had a job as a hairdresser (the other profession open to effeminate men in Costa Rica), but this did not provide her with enough money to live on:

I don't like prostituting myself, but I do it to survive. However, I do like being a transvestite and I like working . . . and most of all I like interacting with people. What I'd really like to do is become a television news announcer. I have a lot of respect for the reporters who read the news. I imagine myself one day sitting beside someone like Amelia Rueda [a prominent radio and television host], giving the weather forecast: "Tomorrow it will be very quiet in the morning, better just stay in bed. By evening, however, your ass will be feeling hot. We recommend cooling it down with some hard cock." I think I'd be really good, really smooth, but who'd ever hire a poor transvestite for a job like that?

DISCRIMINATION AT WORK

One of the key features of transvestism in a country such as Costa Rica is that, for individuals who feel the urge to dress in women's clothing, prostitution is essentially the only avenue open to them. In other words, they are pushed inexorably toward the sex trade by the lack of viable work alternatives. For example, if a transvestite could work in a store or office while dressed in drag, she would be less likely to turn to prostitution. A case in point is Lulu, who worked for a time as a secretary, having convinced her manager that she was in fact a woman:

I was really happy because this was the first time that I was making an honest living, with a real job. The boss didn't know I was a man. At first I didn't really know how to use the typewriter, but after a while I picked it up and then my job was to type in application forms and so on. The trouble started with the clients. They were always inviting me out to have a drink. But I would always say no, just to make sure that no one found out that I was really a man. But one day a driver from work followed me home, and then the next thing I knew he showed up at my house and said that he knew that I was a transvestite and that he'd like to have a fling with me. I told him that I was just a secretary and please don't come to my house anymore. At that point he started to get nasty, but he finally left after I told him to bugger off. Anyway, the next day I find out that he's told the boss, who promptly gave me the pink slip. So that was that, and before you knew it I was back to turning tricks again.

In similar fashion, Pandora also feels that her involvement in the sex trade is largely due to the fact that it has been the only option open to her since she was a child, almost as if dressing in drag and turning tricks went hand in hand.

Finally, one might usefully consider the case of Karina, whose experience is the exception that proves the rule. She is so effeminate that she can easily pass for a woman, and so she has had no difficulty in finding—and keeping—jobs while dressed in drag. As such, she has had no need to turn to the sex trade as a means of supporting herself.

TRANSVESTITES' INCOMES

For the most part, the transvestites interviewed are characterized by low levels of education. Not only have they on average spent a mere 7.4 years in an educational institution, but as many as one third of them (36 percent) have no schooling at all beyond the primary level. Since almost none have learned a trade outside of hairstyling, there is very little potential for them to find meaningful, fulfilling work in their adult lives.

Still, transvestite sex-trade workers enjoy wages that, at first glance, would appear to place them in the lower-middle-class income bracket. In 1990, 59 percent reported earning a monthly income of between 15,000 and 35,000 colones, while 27 percent said that they earned less than 15,000 colones and 14 percent more than 35,000 colones.

However, the fact that more than a quarter of them are making less than 15,000 colones a month, barely a subsistence wage, is disturbing. Out of these earnings, not only must they pay for their food, housing and clothes, but in many cases they hand over a portion to their families as well.

What does it mean to belong to such a poor sector of society? When I asked this question of Karla, she replied, "Being thirsty, seeing a bottle of ice-cold Coke, and not being able to buy it." The transvestites of the Libano district had to content themselves with being surrounded by the middle classes, while being unable to attain such status themselves.

As Louisa put it, "Being poor means being obsessed about money all the time. It's like a drug really. How can I get some? How am I gonna keep it coming?" For others, it is like having the wrong passport, being an illegal alien in one's own country, and thereby becoming, in the words of Cleopatra, "like Indians in the twentieth century, with people hoping you're just going to disappear some day."

Indeed, making matters worse for many of the transvestites is the fact that they have access to the world of wealth and riches through the television set; they can sit in front of it while the host of a cooking show advises them to buy only fresh fruits and vegetables.

"Just imagine how I felt," Chepa recounted, "when Arlene [the host of a cooking program] started groaning about how expensive shrimp were getting. This bothered her so much, she said, that she suggested we only use a quarter kilo in the recipe." Curious, I asked her how she handled this. She answered, "Well, seeing that I don't have a fucking dime to buy shrimp with, I decided to cut back instead on the sweet peppers I was using in their place."

Ana Yanci feels the greatest sense of being poor when she goes to the corner store. "This one time I went to buy some stuff with the money I'd made the night before, and when I got to the counter I realized that I didn't have quite enough to pay for the beans and butter, so I asked the guy, 'Could I put this on my tab?' 'Sure, baby,' he answered, 'just spread your legs so that I can stick my pen up your tab.'"

The johns, for their part, don't tend to be particularly generous either:

> *Hey there sugar, what would you charge to take me up to the sky?*
>
> Well, my dear, that depends. You can get to the sky many ways. What I have to know is how you want to get there, because this flight doesn't come cheap.
>
> *The only way I've gone is by bus. What sort of service are you offering that you're so expensive?*
>
> A trip to Miami for two thousand colones. For this price you'll go first class, and be well-looked after by yours truly.
>
> *What a swindler! It's not as if this is your first trip! I'm sure your motor's seen better days.*
>
> Okay, enough already. You don't have the face of a virgin either. Two thousand colones for the works. Take it or leave it.
>
> *No, baby, listen to me. I'll give you a thousand but I just want a hand job. I don't want a fuck or anything, understand?*
>
> Yeah, whatever. This is low season and I've got a couple openings in my calendar, so I'll give you the discount, but only today . . .
>
> *Yeah, okay, sounds good. But what's this about openings? The only ones I see are where you've got teeth missing.*

Getting a Raise

However, despite the grim picture painted above, it should be emphasized that some transvestites did experience improvement in their standard of living in the early 1990s. The slow shift toward street prostitution, and away from the "bunker" system of the past, afforded transvestites with the opportunity to increase their take-home pay (prostitutes paid commissions to the bunker owners). In the street the latter were better placed to develop relationships with middle- and upper-class clients, who were themselves able to pay a higher price for sex.

"I'll tell you why the rates went up," declared Tirana. "It's really very simple. It's due to a process of globalization, with transvestites suddenly becoming the in thing after Hollywood discovers us and starts making movies about our lives. Then, next thing we know there's more and more rich johns coming down here, wanting to make it with a transvestite themselves."

Troyana, for example, only goes out twice every seven days, with Fridays being the best day of the week, and the fifteenth and thirtieth (i.e., paydays) being the best days of the month. On these occasions, she generally turns four or five tricks during the course of the night, and she is always direct with her clients. "I ask them if they want to give me a blow job, or do they want me to blow them? Do they want to fuck me, or am I gonna fuck them? Or do they want the whole works?"

The rate charged depends upon the type of car the john is driving. For an expensive model, full intercourse costs between 5,000 and 8,000 colones,[1] while oral sex ranges from 1,500 to 2,500 colones. Meanwhile, for a less expensive make of car, the rate is 3,000 to 4,000 colones for full sex, and 1,000 to 1,500 for a blow job. Should the client ask for anything extra, he must pay for it. Typical requests include borrowing the transvestite's clothes or having makeup put on. Sessions can last anywhere from one hour to an hour and a half, with every additional half hour costing 2,500 colones.

Like all the transvestites interviewed, Troyana does not know exactly how much she earns each month, but believes her take-home pay to be between 40,000 and 50,000 colones.

Miriam is known among her colleagues as one of the few transvestites who actually manages to save a portion of her wages, something seldom encountered in the gay sex trade.

Among male prostitutes money is won and lost quickly, with individuals generally being unaware of their relative earnings over time.[2] Many of course feel that the money they make in the sex trade is ill-gotten, and thus spend it quickly in order to ease their own sense of guilt. Moreover, as has already been touched upon, this money is typically spent on luxury items and is rarely invested or saved for future contingencies.

Miriam, from this perspective, is a case apart, having as she does a very keen sense of her savings and earnings. This she attributes to the fact that she loves money: "If someone told me there was five thousand colones lying at the bottom of a cliff, I'd find a way of going down there and getting it." For the most part, she goes out to work every night, turning an average of five tricks each time, though "sometimes I'll go out and won't make a dime, won't even be given the time of day." Still, she claims to make between 95,000 and 100,000 colones in a poor month, and that her average monthly salary is as much as 150,000 colones, of which she invests roughly half.

Like her colleagues, she spends about an hour with each client, for which she charges 5,000 colones, or 2,500 to 3,000 colones if oral sex is all that is desired. Special requests, as always, cost extra.

Colirio also reports seeing an average of five clients per night and, like Troyana, sets her rates according to the type of car the john drives: "Generally, if they pull up in a Mercedes I'll charge them more. But if they seem nice, and treat me well, I'll sometimes go easy and give them a break."

On average, however, she charges between 6,000 and 7,000 colones for intercourse, and 2,500 and 3,000 for blow jobs. Also like many of the others, she does not keep records of her earnings: "No, I don't really keep track, but on a good day I clear about ten thousand colones, and on a really good day maybe twice that."

She is also asked from time to time to participate in sex shows with another transvestite, or with a *zorra* (a gay male prostitute who dresses in men's clothing). For these, which are usually put on either for a single client or for a couple, she charges between 15,000 and 20,000 colones, with any additional services costing extra.

Elena notes that she will sometimes get a john who will pay her from 10,000 to 20,000 colones over the course of one night and, though she admits that this is quite rare, there have even been occasions when she has been paid 30,000 or, once, 85,000 colones for a single night's work.

Several interview participants indicated that, in the transvestite community, there is a tendency to exaggerate earnings as a way of enhancing one's image. Thus, while media accounts of transvestite prostitution in San José have reported monthly earnings ranging from 350,000 to 400,000 colones, such figures are described as highly overblown by transvestites such as Miriam, who is among the city's highest earners.

Price Cutters

Among the reasons for the wide variation in the rates transvestites charge their clients is the practice of *hacer cuechas* (spitting), or price cutting. Few are held in higher contempt by their colleagues than those who engage in such rate cutting. To quote Elena, "In the ten blocks that we work, you'll see everything: hot bodies, good makeup jobs, exotic looks, expensive wigs, the works. The transvestite who charges less undermines all this, and makes us lose clients."

Cuechas involves charging a discounted rate for the same service: 1,500 to 2,000 colones for intercourse (the usual price is 5,000 colones) and 500 colones for oral sex.

Little that is positive is said about those who give *cuechas*. Miriam, for one, describes them in the following terms: "They're dicks without eyes. I charge my clients five thousand colones while they're taking them on for five hundred. . . . They're just looking for a place to shoot their wad; they're not selective at all. I wouldn't even say that this is competition; it's merely a question of standing there, offering oneself, and being lucky."

Elena feels the same way: "There's always someone who'll undercut you and this is the worst sort of competition. I had a client once who left me for someone who cut her rates. . . . It didn't bother me though, it wasn't because of me he left."

Improvement in Income

In Mabé's opinion, she is earning considerably more from prostitution now than she was in the past. However, as she put it, "The johns pay more but at the same time they want women who are more beautiful. There's no way they'd go for the sort of she-monsters who hang out around the Libano cinema. Now they want transvestites who look like movie stars."

That there is more money flowing through the transvestite community is obvious. In place of the cheap clothes, wigs, and makeup of the past, the transvestites are wearing outfits imported from the United States, wigs made from real hair, professional makeup, and expensive perfume. Transvestites such as Pili have even been able to afford the luxury of silicone breast implants: "These tits cost me a fortune. I used to inject hormones but finally decided to have surgery instead." Corella has had her body hair removed, her nose straightened, and her teeth whitened, while Marlene has invested in liposuction to improve the appearance of her waist.

Needless to say, recent changes in transvestites' physical appearance are closely related to the johns' growing appetite for glamorous "women." Like Mabé, Lulu reports that her clients want prostitutes who remind them of movie stars. "However, Costa Rican women are all small with big hips. Only men who are tall and thin can give them the sort of phenomenal body they're looking for."

Thus, when one looks at a transvestite such as Sharon, one sees a woman who is very tall, with the sort of body that would be at home on a catwalk. "Look, the bottom line is that there's no middle-class hooker out there who looks as glamorous as me. Men turn around to look at me, whether they're into transvestites or not," she said with pride. Angelita, meanwhile, feels that the competence of female sex-trade workers is generally "very low." As she put it, "The prostitutes are all old and fat, they've got children, and they come cheaply."

REASONS FOR TRANSVESTITES' SUCCESS

It should be emphasized that it is not merely on account of their physical appearance that the transvestites deem themselves superior to the female prostitutes, but also, paradoxically, by virtue of the fact that they are men. In short, they feel that their male gender gives them particular insight into the bodies and desires of their customers. Thus, Penelope stressed that she knows what men want and, "Because I'm a man, I touch men differently." That is to say, she believes that female sex-trade workers do not know how to engage in oral sex, masturbate, or penetrate men in the way that the men themselves would like. They don't know "how a man wants them to talk, to respond, or to act in bed." A similar view is expressed by Lola, who argues that "a guy doesn't have to tell me what he'd like me to do. Since I've got a body just like his, I know exactly what to do to drive him wild."

Of course, it bears emphasizing as well that the transvestite is not merely selling the sex act itself, but also something of a "show." Thus, many will model themselves, put on an act, or sing for the client before they engage in physical contact. Knowledgeable of men's wishes and desires, they can exploit these as a way of earning thousands of extra colones, while the client has the opportunity of having his most secret fantasy fulfilled. For instance, Eva charges 10,000 colones to pretend she is a nanny who is about to be raped by her man of the house. Esther, meanwhile, plays the part of Marilyn Monroe, even dressing herself up similarly. Kristina puts on a show in which she pretends to be Gloria Estefan, charging her clients 13,000 colones each time. Finally, Fresa likes to play the role of a nun, and even has a habit and rosary on hand to make her act seem more realistic.

Still, despite this apparent bonanza, few transvestites have managed to improve their position in life as a result. As we will see in the next chapter, drug addiction robs them of much of their earnings, as do their lovers and the police. By the time they are old enough to appreciate the importance of saving a portion of their earnings, they are usually too old to be deemed attractive by the johns. Thus, at the end of the day their dreams of fame and riches pass them by, and they are left to die of AIDS in the same neighborhood they had left ten years previously, holed up in one of the grim bunkers around the Libano cinema.

Chapter 7

Drugs

That so many of the transvestites consume drugs should not be particularly surprising. If we were the ones prostituting ourselves in their place, receiving the taunts, the attacks, and the insults that they do on a daily basis, we would surely resort to drug abuse ourselves, as a way of insulating ourselves from the homophobic culture that surrounds us.

Why do you use drugs, Pepa?

Standing on a corner by myself, waiting to see who's going to pass by and not knowing who it's going to be, if I'm going to end up raped, stabbed, or dead, makes me feel extremely anxious. Every time a car goes by I don't know if I'm going to be pelted with shit or invited to go dancing. It's like being Cinderella, but in reverse. I don't know whether I'll end up marrying the prince or some old fart. Anyway, it's because of this that I feel the need to get stoned. When I'm really ripped, and people start shouting obscenities at me, all I can hear are praises: "shit-faced whore" becomes "beautiful rose"; "butt-fucking dog" becomes "what a lovely hat"; "demon seed" becomes "sweet pea" and, in the end, I couldn't care less what they're yelling. Or, if they throw a stone at me, I pick it up and it looks just like a sweet little flower; a bag of piss sprayed on me feels like a blessing with holy water; a rotten egg becomes a bouquet of roses. If they put me in jail, it's like I'm vacationing in the Caribbean, or if I'm raped, I tell myself it's just an aerobics workout.

Do you find the drugs make it easier not to see the homophobia?

It's not that I can't see it, just that it bothers me less. Do you really think it's possible not to notice it when they start yelling at you as soon as they see you're dressed as a woman? Going out on the street is very difficult. You've got have lots of balls to do it. In order to live like this, not knowing where the next attack's coming from, you've got to get ripped. If you don't, you're going to feel like shit all over.

Who's responsible then for the fact that you use drugs?

I'm not going to say that it's all their fault. But a large part of it is due to the fact that they're at us all the time. They never leave us in peace. What the fuck have we done to deserve these attacks? Why is it that there's no human rights organization out there that's speaking out against the abuse we receive?

Clearly, Pepa is not alone is her use of drugs:

I spend about 4500 colones per month on smokes, 24,000 on alcohol, and about four to eight thousand on coke. In a month drugs will cost me about 30,000 to 36,000 colones. When I've got drugs I share them with my friends from work. The johns will also offer them to me, over and above the money they're paying. (Leticia)

I'm into marijuana. It costs me about one hundred to two hundred colones a day. I've been smoking it pretty much continuously ever since I first started. I've tried various drugs and have used some on a regular basis, but I really prefer weed. If I'm going to a party I may spend as much as ten thousand on it. (Susy)

CRACK IS KING

In carrying out interviews with members of the transvestite community, the project ethnographer established that crack has been the drug of choice since roughly the 1980s. It is made by mixing cocaine, bicarbonate of soda, and water in a spoon, and then heating it over a candle, stirring it continuously with a match. Once the contents have begun to boil, the heat is removed, and the mixture is stirred until it has coalesced into a hard rock.

The rock is broken into pieces, which are placed inside an empty plastic juice bottle in which holes have been made. Users burn the pieces one at a time and inhale the smoke deeply until the rock is entirely consumed.

The bottles are jealously guarded. Those who do not have them use cups half filled with water, with aluminum foil on top. They inhale the smoke through holes in the foil. This method is considered inferior, though, because the water absorbs part of the drug as it burns.

BASUKO

Another popular drug is called *basuko,* made from a combination of marijuana and cocaine. In effect, it involves sprinkling cocaine (in powder form) over the marijuana as one rolls it into a joint; it is then smoked as though it were a normal cigarette.

Needless to say, for those frequenting discotheques it is difficult to smoke drugs discreetly. In the face of this dilemma, and given that marijuana produces such a strong odor when consumed, many will simply remove the tobacco from regular cigarettes, mix cocaine into it, and then reinsert the adulterated tobacco so that they might smoke it later without attracting any attention. Of course, the majority prefer cocaine in any case, and thus will either smoke it in the manner described above (called a *rayita* in local parlance), or snort a line in the bathroom when no one is watching.

Conversely, there are many who will simply consume all of the evening's drugs at once, before going out, to avoid carrying with them anything that might later be found by the police.

However, when transvestites do carry cocaine (e.g., to sell), they will often do so by placing a quarter gram in a *pajilla*, a piece of plastic that has been heat-sealed. This in turn they will put in their mouths, to avoid detection should they be searched.

In the Libano district, drugs were sold in various locales, with the drug dealer generally being the one who buys the pure cocaine in bulk and then mixes it with crushed-up amphetamines and tranquilizers. When the ethnographer visited the area's brothels and rooming houses in 1990, he had the opportunity to see the drug preparation process unfold on several occasions, from the mixing of the cocaine in a blender to the packaging of individual "hits" (wrapped in cigarette foil) for retail sale.

Meanwhile, when it comes to smoking marijuana, those who are unable to obtain a *boleta* (rolling paper for cigarettes that is sold in stores in the vicinity of San José's Central Market) will often use wrapping paper from bread or toilet paper instead. Of course, also critical in this regard is the *matadora,* a piece of bamboo that has been hollowed and split, and used to smoke the final portion of the joint without burning one's fingers.

When the ethnographer carried out his interviews with drug-consuming transvestites in 1990, none of them held out much hope of overcoming their addictions. Even if they found themselves without money, they would go out for a walk and within twenty minutes they would have stolen something that could be given to their dealer or "doctor" (so-called because of his "prescriptions") in exchange for drugs.

Unfortunately, the situation in 1997 in the Clinica Biblica area appear to be even worse. Very few transvestites working there are not substance abusers in some form or fashion. Although the bunkers of the Libano district are no longer the centers of supply that they once were, drugs are easily bought elsewhere, whether in individuals' homes, tenement complexes, or on the street.

Changes in transvestites' physical appearance are also evident: not only is basic bodily care being neglected, but crack consumption has also caused many addicts to lose a significant portion of their body mass. Some, such as Peggy, who have always been heavyset, are now extremely skinny, something which she blames on the "bottle" (i.e., crack use). She also suffers from a bad cough, and says that her lungs were deemed to be in poor shape following a recent exam undertaken at INISA.[1] Needless to say, she is not alone in this: constant coughing and a gaunt, cadaverous appearance are ubiquitous among crack-consuming members of the transvestite community. Significantly, a few of those interviewed said that they took crack as a means of making themselves look like fashion models, though of course at the cost of slowly destroying their bodies from the inside out. Of the 100 transvestites working the Clinica Biblica area on a regular basis, seventy-five are considered crack abusers.

SEX AND DRUGS

Studies undertaken in other countries have shown that those who engage in substance use during or before sexual relations are more likely to practice unsafe sex. In the particular case of the transvestite community, 68 percent indicated that they had consumed alcohol at some point in their lives. The rates are even higher for other substances. For example, 77 percent report being marijuana smokers, with 76 percent of the latter stating that they use it either somewhat or very often before sex, and 53 percent indicating that they use it very often. As for cocaine, 73 percent of those questioned had tried it. However, it should be noted that none of the transvestites interviewed reported consuming drugs intravenously.[2]

The transvestites' consumption of drugs—particularly cocaine, marijuana and crack—is significantly related to the type of work in which they are engaged. Not only is prostitution an activity that requires a great deal of physical exertion, but it also demands of the individual a psychological orientation in which one is able to detach oneself emotionally from the trauma associated with the job. When this is combined with near-continuous harassment on the part of the police and general public, drugs serve as a way of anesthetizing oneself from the pain.

Apparently, both crack and cocaine are used principally to enhance sexual performance or make it possible to engage in sex more frequently. Marlene highlighted this by indicating that "coke helps me make love," while marijuana serves only to "distract me." A similar point of view was expressed by Julie, who believes that cocaine makes her "more exciting . . . crazier in bed." Marijuana, by contrast, does not appeal to her at all. Patricia stated that although she is not strongly attracted to any drug in particular, she does like cocaine, which she takes so as "not to feel alone."

> I've made love when I'm high. I like to do it while I'm on coke. It feels great just after I've done it; I can make love and nothing bothers me. The feeling lasts up to two hours; when I smoke it, I enjoy sex even more.

Adelita feels that, despite the fact that coke can make one "crazier" in bed, it does have a number of drawbacks:

> Just because you're a transvestite doesn't mean you do lots of drugs. I don't smoke anything. I've tried them but I don't like them. The johns do drugs; once I had sex with this guy who had some coke on him and I did some. When he kissed me and stuck his tongue in my mouth, it felt really big, and then he started touching me with his penis and it felt huge, and when he put in my rectum it felt really big in there. I enjoyed it, but I can't say it really excited me. I believe drugs make you hornier but they destroy you from the inside, and you lose control in bed.

Along somewhat different lines, Apolonia was quite adamant in stressing that "nothing makes sex better than coke." Others, meanwhile, felt that marijuana was more stimulating. Marlene, for one, indicated that she really got into sex after she had smoked it, while Susy said that, because cocaine often prevents her from ejaculating, she prefers marijuana, which "gives a better buzz and makes me hornier." Still other interview participants indicated that they preferred beer and alcohol. Finally, a few transvestites, Gina and Karla in particular, said that although they have tried drugs, they almost never consume them.

However, one of the most serious problems with substance use in the community is that it causes individuals to take risks and engage in unsafe sex. For example, Susy indicated that when she is under the effects of drugs she is less likely to wear a condom:

> I've been really high and really turned on and then, when it's time to put a condom on, I've just left it aside and carried on without even thinking about it.

Still, it should also be noted that others, such as Julie, have stressed that they continue to practice safe sex even when they are high.

Thus, even though our research in 1997 did not focus specifically on the issue of drugs, not only was it clear that there had been no decline in transvestites' substance use over the course of the past decade, one might even say that there has been something of an increase.

It also bears emphasizing that there has recently been a marked increase in the number of transvestite drug abusers enrolling in ILPES's detoxication services. Many come to ask for food or money from staff working with the institute's prevention programs, such as Group 2828 and the Priscilla Project. Others have gone back to spend their last days in one of the old bunkers of the Libano district. As one might imagine, AIDS has taken a heavy toll within this community, with dozens of men dying from complications associated with the disease over the past decade.

Chapter 8

Top-Man, Bottom-Man

As one might imagine, members of San José's transvestite community have an elevated number of sexual contacts as a result of their line of work. When we asked them in 1990 how many sexual partners they had had during their lives (see Table 8.1), the average response was 9,371 and, for the prior five-year period only, the response was 4,835.4. During the previous twelve months the average number of partners was 830.4, or 15.9 per week. Finally, for the previous thirty days, respondents indicated that they had had (on average) 44.8 partners, or 11.2 per week. These figures have not changed significantly over the past seven years.

Although these numbers may appear excessively high at first glance, they were corroborated by transvestites' responses in the in-depth interview sessions. That is to say, not only was it common for participants to have up to a dozen sexual encounters over a weekend, but some reported having as many six partners in one night.

If we assume that there are 100 to 150 transvestites working in San José at any given moment in time (this estimate is for the city as a whole, and is derived from the reports of transvestites themselves) and that each has an average of four partners per night, this means that as many as 600 men are using their services every day.

However, because the johns do not always return to the same prostitute, it is difficult to calculate with any certainty the number of visits they are making on a weekly, monthly, or annual basis.

In 1990 we also asked transvestites to report on the degree of satisfaction they associated with various sexual practices, assuming that there was no danger of HIV infection. As Table 8.2 suggests,

TABLE 8.1. Average Number and Sex of Partners, and Degree of Certainty Regarding Numbers Cited

Variable		Gay	Transvestite sex-trade workers
	(N)	(162)	(22)
	Total	100	100
Sexual partners			
Over lifetime		497	9,371
Women		1.8	0.09
Men		495	9,370
Last five years		157.5	4,835.4
Women		0.8	—
Men		156.7	4,835.4
Last twelve months		18.5	830.4
Women		0.1	—
Men		18.4	830.4
Last thirty days		2.2	44.8
Women		0.01	—
Men		2.2	44.8
Occasional (nonregular)			
Women		3.5	35.2
Men		3.5	22.9
Degree of certainty regarding above figures:			
Last twelve months			
Very certain		46.3	4.5
Certain		28.4	31.8
Neither certain nor uncertain		21.6	59.1
Uncertain		1.2	—
Very uncertain		2.6	4.5
Last thirty days			
Very certain		84.0	45.5
Certain		13.6	40.9
Neither certain nor uncertain		—	13.6
Uncertain		0.6	—

Source: Jacobo Schifter and Johnny Madrigal, *Hombres que Aman Hombres,* San José, Costa Rica, ILEP-SIDA, 1992.

TABLE 8.2. Degree of Excitement Associated with Various Sexual Practices (Percent)

Variable	Gay	Transvestite sex-trade workers
(N)	(162)	(22)
Total	100	100
Receiving fellatio from a man, until ejaculation		
Very exciting	79.6	72.7
Somewhat exciting	10.5	13.6
Neutral	4.9	—
Somewhat unpleasant	0.6	—
Very unpleasant	3.7	4.5
Unsure	0.6	9.1
Removing penis before ejaculation		
Very exciting	49.4	54.5
Somewhat exciting	28.4	18.2
Neutral	9.9	—
Somewhat unpleasant	6.2	4.5
Very unpleasant	4.9	9.1
Unsure	1.2	13.6
Penetrating a man's anus, until ejaculation		
Very exciting	74.7	90.9
Somewhat exciting	10.5	—
Neutral	8.0	—
Somewhat unpleasant	1.9	4.5
Very unpleasant	2.5	—
Unsure	2.5	4.5
While using a condom		
Very exciting	41.4	72.7
Somewhat exciting	18.5	4.5
Neutral	19.1	—
Somewhat unpleasant	9.9	4.5
Very unpleasant	8.0	4.5
Unsure	3.1	13.6
Being penetrated in the anus by a man, until ejaculation		
Very exciting	56.8	68.2
Somewhat exciting	13.0	13.6
Neutral	10.5	4.5
Somewhat unpleasant	8.0	4.5
Very unpleasant	6.8	9.1
Unsure	4.9	—

Source: Jacobo Schifter and Johnny Madrigal, *Hombres que Aman Hombres*, San José, Costa Rica, ILEP-SIDA, 1992.

the overwhelming majority of respondents (91 percent) found active anal penetration to be most exciting. In somewhat fewer cases (68 percent), passive anal penetration was considered equally exciting. Thus, contrary to dominant prejudices and stereotypes, this means that transvestites prefer to play the role of the "man" more often than that of the "woman." Simply put, they enjoy penetrating their clients.

And what about the johns? In 1997 we asked Sonia Marta to tell us about her clients and what they like to do. In her response, she emphasized the degree of variability in their tastes. We also asked her to tape record a typical sexual encounter (with the consent of the client in question).

According to her, the men who use her services are not homosexual. Like other transvestites, she describes her clients as "macho" men who are into women rather than men. As Sonia put it, "They're not fags. They're real men, married with children, average guys really." She stressed that she would never have sex with a homosexual man.

In this way, despite the fact that the majority of the clientele would have absolutely nothing to do with the Costa Rican gay community, they might be classified as bisexual, albeit with certain qualifications. In general, most of them would not have sexual relations with men who are dressed as men. They are attracted to the feminine in men and not to both sexes.

A SEXUAL ENCOUNTER

Sonia Marta asked several of her clients whether she could tape record one of their sessions. Only one consented, and did so on the condition that the recording would be erased after it was transcribed. What follows is a condensed version of the recording:

What do you charge, baby?

Five thousand colones for whatever you want. But I've been asked to tape the session for three thousand colones, so if you're okay with it, I'll only charge you two thousand. It's a promotional offer.

What's the recording for? Are you taping right now?

[She stops recording and then starts the machine again.]

It's for a friend of mine who's writing a book. He'll write down what's said, and then erase the tape.

Okay, it doesn't bother me. Anyway, I like the idea of putting on a show. But nothing about men, and no talk about my car or about me.

Sounds good. Listen, don't worry; I could've put the tape player in my bag—you see it's small enough—without you even noticing. I'm telling you this just so you know there's nothing going on.

What do you like to do?

It depends on the client, though I do prefer to be the one doing it really.

Good, get in the car. What's your name?

Sonia Marta.

And how long have you been working here?

About a year and a half.

I've never seen you before.

It's probably because I'm not here every night.

So, sweetheart, where are we going?

I'd prefer a motel. How about El Paraiso?

Sounds good, but I want you to keep your head down when we go in, okay?

Yeah, okay.

Those tits, are they real?

Yeah, I've had them for a while.

How long have you been a transvestite?

I've been into dressing up like a woman since I was little; I started when I was about six.

And what is it that you like as a woman?

I'm into men and I want them to treat me either like a lady or a whore.

What do you like in men? What do you think when you look at me?

Well, I like men who are masculine and manly, like yourself. Has anyone told you that you're very handsome?

Well yes, actually. I'm usually lucky with the ladies.

Are you married?

Yeah, for four years.

So what is it that you're looking for in me then?

I'm into rough, hard sex. I like women who are hot, aggressive, savage, and adventurous in bed.

And how do you know that I'm like that?

It's because you've got such hot lips and such a hard, tight butt. Girls' asses drive me wild. Touch my dick; make it hard.

What an animal! Is this all you? You're very well endowed.

Do you like it? It's all for you. You're going to eat it all.

I'm going to open your zipper and take it out. Is that okay?

Yeah but be careful; we're close to the police station right now.

[Sound of groaning for a few seconds.]

Sweet thing! If you carry on like that we're not gonna make it to the hotel. Better stop for a minute. Baby, that was really good.

It's that I really like you. You're a very strong, handsome man. Have you ever been told that you have beautiful eyes?

Uh-uh.

What do you have in mind for the motel? What would you like me to do?

When we get there, I'd like you to wash first 'cause I like it when my girls smell good. Next, I'll order something to eat and drink and I want you to come out wearing some lingerie. You don't have to hide anything baby 'cause I know what you've got between your legs and it doesn't bother me.

That sounds good, and since you already know the truth, I'll say again how much I like doing it to the johns, especially when they're manly like you. Touch my cock, put your hand here. Do you see I'm also quite well-developed?

What a size! Who would've known that you're so big?

That's why I have so many clients. They like a well-endowed woman.

So do I, baby. Being in bed with a female who's so well-equipped drives me crazy. Look, we're almost there. Put your head down so they don't see you.

[Sound of the john going to the telephone and ordering liquor, snacks, lubricant, and condoms.]

Go to the bathroom and start washing. Soap yourself really well. I'll wait here for the food and drinks. Also, I'm going to start taking off my clothes, because I like being comfortable. Do you know what I mean?

Yeah, of course.

[Music and, in the background, the shower running. After a few minutes, the doorbell rings, announcing the arrival of the supplies.]

I'm all clean and washed. Where are you? Oh you brute, you're already undressed!

Come over here, darling. Before we eat, I want you to take this and put it in your mouth. Yeah, just like that. What a tongue, babe! Who taught you to lick like a little dog? Oh, you're a stud, you're a beast . . . !

Should I take off my panties?

Take off anything you like, darling; let me look at your cock. First I'm going to punish you for being a naughty girl. Then, I want you to put this lubricant on the condom and stick it on me. Stop there in front of the mirror so I can see you from behind.

[Since we're taping this, I just wanted to tell our audience that he's going in little by little, very carefully.]

It's not hurting, right? It's really tight, just like a virgin. What are you feeling, sweetheart?

I can really feel it, you fiend. It's hurting a lot. Ouch, don't move like that!

Don't move an inch. Let me do everything. Get up from the bed and we'll go like this, just like two dogs, in front of the mirror.

Okay, that's good.

Now we're going to change roles and you'll do it to me. Put on the condom and some lubricant. Careful, there's no hurry. Now do it slowly, don't be rough—do it like I did it to you.

Bend over a bit more so that I can do it right, and don't move.

Oh, that feels so good! Darling, you're a lady who knows how to do things right! Move a bit now, but slowly. I've always thought that women know how to fuck since they're the ones who are usually on the receiving end. Isn't that right? Do it like I did it to you, you know how. There, that's the way to do it. Oh, that's nice! Be careful the condom doesn't come off.

[Groans and cries of pleasure until both attain orgasm a few minutes later.]

TRANSVESTITES ARE NOT PASSIVE PARTNERS

Throughout the qualitative interviews, it was shown that transvestites, with few exceptions, practice either active or passive anal intercourse (and sometimes both) with regular clients. Indeed, one of the reasons why the johns—the majority of whom are married or single men who deem themselves to be exclusively heterosexual—seek out transvestite lovers in the first place is because they see the latter as women with penises. This in turn explains why active intercourse on the part of the transvestites is as popular among the clients as it is. While admittedly there are some transvestites who do not enjoy penetrating other men, these are the minority. Given the frequency with which they are asked to engage in such penetration, even those who do not enjoy it do it anyway for the sake of business.

Roxana, for example, stressed that in her profession "there are those who like to be active," even though she does not. Julieta shares this opinion, though she admitted that, in her case, what clients like best about her is her penis, and that "married clients in particular tell me how much they like it." Gloria indicated that "there are some johns who like to make love and others who want me to do it," with the latter being principally "older or married men." Similarly, Karla emphasized that "most of the johns who want me to be the active partner are those who are married, divorced, or bachelors." As for Stephanie, she said that the clients enjoy being penetrated by her, and that "they know who they're dealing with." In any case, she prefers to be active rather than passive. Carla, meanwhile, described it thus: "There are men who, the first time you do it with them, you think they're all man, but then they get into bed and they start acting like a whore. I tell them to lean forward and I start at it. . . . I prefer the more masculine men, but they're all the same." Antonieta also believes that the majority of her clients would "like me to fuck them" and that it is in any case better to be the active partner than the passive one. Along similar lines, Marlene indicated that it doesn't bother her "when I go to bed with a masculine man who then asks me to fuck him." Pandora also has a number of married clients with children who like it "when I make love with them." Finally, Julie noted that, among her ten regular clients (most of whom are married), although most had insisted that they play the active role initially, this soon changed:

> At first, they were looking for somebody who'd be the woman; now I'm the man and they're playing the part of the woman. This has changed because they're feeling more comfortable; you'd think they were masculine men by looking at them, but in bed they become feminine women. . . . They want me to penetrate them about 80 percent of the time. At first I didn't like it, but I've got used to it.

Despite the fact that the transvestites are more likely to use condoms than many other marginalized groups, it is clear that their sexual relations do involve considerable risk. This is the case both because of the frequency of penetration (whether active or passive) and the number of occasions when they fail to use a prophylactic. In short, even though many have begun to practice safe sex, the continuing prevalence of unsafe practices among some transvestites places the community in a high-risk situation.

Most of the transvestites queried did not feel that the use of a condom diminishes the pleasure associated with sex. Indeed, rather the reverse: 82 percent of participants found active anal sex more exciting while wearing a condom, as compared to 77 percent who found it equally exciting while not wearing one. Thus, it is clear that respondents enjoy sex less when they are not using a condom, a finding that may be explained by individuals' fears of contracting HIV in the process (see Table 8.2).

This discrepancy is even more obvious when one considers the case of passive anal sex. If a condom is used, as many as 82 percent of participants find it very exciting, whereas only 59 percent find it equally so when their partner is not using one.

LOVE AND CONDOMS DON'T MIX

Still, additional research on condom use among transvestites shows that they tend to be more disposed not to use one should their partner express a desire not to.[1] A large majority of respondents (86 percent) indicated that the identity of the partner (i.e., a lover or a stranger) was a factor in the decision about whether to use a condom.

Clearly, this is an important finding, underscoring as it does the fact that transvestites are more likely to practice unsafe sex with lovers or habitual partners. Needless to say, this constitutes a significant risk factor. As will be shown, the reason for this behavior can be traced to the type of personal bonds that are established outside of the sex trade.

Condoms

As our interviews with the transvestites clearly show, the latter have for the most part continued to engage in their preferred sexual practices, including masturbation and active and passive penetration, without any modification other than the incorporation of condoms into their sexual repertoire. The majority indicated that condom use posed no serious obstacle to their enjoyment of sex, a fact that is itself closely related to transvestites' willingness to make use of it in the first place. However, there are some exceptions. Various transvestites reported feeling a profound repulsion toward condoms, with Leticia being but one example:

> With condoms, whether you use one, two, or three, you tend to get cuts. For me, condoms are like Chinese water torture, because blowing somebody off with one is like eating a candy with the wrapper still on, or a banana without peeling it. But the fact is that I've got to use one, though I wish there was something else that I could use instead.

Susy expressed a similar point of view:

> Some condoms, I find, are too small, and so it doesn't feel as good. Also, if I'm going to be giving someone a blow job, I ask them to use a nonlubricated one, because some of them taste really bad.

Still, it is clear from the in-depth interviews that the transvestites understood the value of condom use. Carla, for example, stressed that she has used them ever since AIDS first appeared, in spite of the fact that "clients say they can't feel anything. It's better to use one than die."

Along similar lines, Gina stated that she used one "because I have to" and "because AIDS is a disease that kills, so I protect myself with a condom." Such a perspective was also evident in Karina's words, "Condoms are useful because they're the only the way to avoid catching AIDS."

Still, it is clear that there are several forces which may work to frustrate the good intentions expressed above. At the most basic level, condoms do occasionally rip. Indeed, as many as 91 percent of respondents indicated that, in their experience, condoms tore easily during sex.[2]

One explanation for this finding is that since the transvestites have a relatively large number of sexual encounters, the likelihood of a condom ripping increases. Also relevant in this regard is the fact that transvestites often engage in anal sex, which is considered more likely to produce torn condoms than vaginal intercourse (studies have shown that condoms rip in 2 percent of cases of vaginal penetration, compared with 10 percent of cases of anal penetration). Not only is this exacerbated by the tendency among transvestites to use cheap, low-quality condoms that are more susceptible to tearing, but in many cases, neither they nor their partners know how to use them correctly. As Hatcher and Hughes have demonstrated, condoms are most prone to ripping when they are used by individuals who are unaccustomed to them.[3]

Still, whatever the reason, the fact remains that condom failure places both the transvestite and her partner at risk. Awareness of this danger is apparent in the in-depth interviews.

For instance, Apolonia stated that "I don't like condoms. They burst and then they're no protection at all, so I usually use three or four at once." A similar point of view was expressed by Julie, who said, "It upsets me when they break, because that means we're no longer safe." Marlene paid dearly for condom failure on one occasion when she "slept with a guy and the condom ripped, and then few days later I started feeling poor, and in the end it came out that I'd caught gonorrhea." Patricia also indicated that "condoms have burst on me more than once."

Client Reluctance to Use Condoms

Another obstacle in the way of safe sex is the client himself. During the course of the qualitative interviews, it was shown that johns often attempt to induce the transvestites not to use condoms, for example by offering them more money. Consider the following statement by Carla: "Some clients don't want to use condoms because they don't like the feel of them, even though it's the only way of avoiding diseases. Some will even offer me extra not to use them." Gina admitted that there have been cases when she has not used them in return for higher payment: "If they say, 'I'll give you money not to wear one,' I'll generally agree, though I first check them to make sure they look clean." By contrast, Karina said that even when she is offered more money, she usually insists that one be used anyway: "They [the clients] don't like it, but they put it on.

'No glove, no love,' even though it doesn't feel the same." Similarly, Patricia stated that "Even if a john told me that he'd pay double not to use a condom, I'd rather not earn anything than earn something just to die quickly."

Julie has something of a double standard. If she knows the client and he is willing to pay more, she will agree not to use one; however, if the client is new, she will insist on condoms, regardless of whether he wants to use them. As she put it, "There's guys around who don't like using them. If I've known them for years, I won't use one. But if it's a new client, he could offer twice as much money not to use one, but I still wouldn't do it." Along similar lines, Marcela also bases her decision on the degree of trust she has in her partner: "If I trust the john, and he looks okay when I check him out with the lights on, I'll do it without a condom." Leticia indicated that she would agree not to use one in cases where "the guy drives me wild."

As for Karla, she said that she would not use a condom if the client was "sweet," or if he had money and she "knows what sort of life he leads." Gloria is willing not to use one if the client pays more, but will only do so for oral sex. Similarly, Julieta does not insist on their use in cases where the client agrees to pay more, but only if "I trust the person and he looks okay." Finally, Pandora resolves the question of whether she should use a condom by engaging in something of a ruse:

> Since a lot of clients don't like wearing one when they're making love, I'll either put it on them while we're making love without them noticing, or else I trick them by not letting them penetrate me I simply put it between my legs. They think it's inside of me, and I start going through the motions, saying how hot it feels and how it's hurting, just so they think they're really doing it.

Of course, it need hardly be emphasized that drug consumption is another factor that may cause individuals not to use a condom, with Fabiola providing but one example:

> There have been times that I've not used a condom because I'm stoned. There was this one time that I was in a bar, I took a

Roche pill, and then we went home. I don't remember a thing. A friend told me later that I'd done it with three men, one after the other, and I was so out of it that either the condom broke or I didn't use one in the first place.

Still, this is not to say that substance use need necessarily lead to unsafe sex, as Leticia's partner made clear:

I use a condom, even when I'm stoned. I always use one. We have sex once or twice a week. One time I didn't wear one and it felt uncomfortable because I generally always do.

UNSAFE SEX REMAINS A PROBLEM

In 1990, the percentage of transvestites who had engaged in unsafe sexual practices over the course of the previous thirty days was high (see Table 8.3).

At this time, 59 percent of respondents reported having oral sex, 41 percent active anal sex, and 46 percent passive anal sex without a condom. If one examines these figures as they pertain to the previous six months (see Table 8.4), one finds 50 percent of transvestites practicing active anal penetration, and 59 percent passive anal penetration without using a condom.

This in turn means that, in 1990, as many as half of those queried had had unsafe sex during the previous six months. While admittedly we did not undertake a similar study of safe sex practices in 1997, the qualitative interviews carried out with transvestites show that the level of condom use has increased in this community, and that they are almost always used during commercial sex. At the same time, however, many admitted making "exceptions" when they were very intoxicated or with their lovers.

TABLE 8.3. Inventory of Sexual Practices and Average Number of Occurrences in the Past Thirty Days (Percent)

Variable		Gay	Transvestite sex-trade workers
	(N)	(162)	(22)
	Total	100	100
Have you penetrated a woman through the anus?			
Without ejaculation		—	4.6
Until ejaculation		—	—
With condom		—	—
Without condom		—	4.6
Removing the penis before ejaculation		—	4.6
Have you penetrated a man?			
Without ejaculation		29.0	72.7
Until ejaculation		53.7	72.7
With condom		49.4	86.4
Without condom		22.8	40.9
Removing the penis before ejaculation		17.3	45.4
Have you been penetrated by a man?			
Without ejaculation		23.5	56.4
Until ejaculation		42.6	77.3
With condom		40.7	95.5
Without condom		17.9	45.5
Removing the penis before ejaculation		16.7	40.9
Have you penetrated a woman through the vagina?			
Without ejaculation		0.6	4.6
Until ejaculation		1.2	—
With condom		0.6	—
Without condom		1.2	—
Removing the penis before ejaculation		—	4.6
Have you stimulated orally . . .			
A woman?		—	—
A man?		45.1	27.3

Source: Jacobo Schifter and Johnny Madrigal, *Hombres que Aman Hombres*, San José, Costa Rica, ILEP-SIDA, 1992.

TABLE 8.4. Inventory of Sexual Practices During the Past Six Months (Percent)

Variable		Gay	Transvestite sex-trade workers
	(N)	(162)	(22)
	Total	100	100
Have you penetrated a woman through the anus?			
Without ejaculation		0.6	9.1
Until ejaculation		0.6	—
With condom		1.2	—
Without condom		0.6	4.5
Removing the penis before ejaculation		1.2	4.5
Have you penetrated a man?			
Without ejaculation		61.1	86.4
Until ejaculation		75.9	90.9
With condom		73.5	90.9
Without condom		37.0	50.5
Removing the penis before ejaculation		38.9	72.7
Have you been penetrated by a man?			
Without ejaculation		56.2	86.4
Until ejaculation		65.4	86.4
With condom		67.9	95.5
Without condom		37.7	59.1
Removing the penis before ejaculation		37.7	72.7
Have you penetrated a woman through the vagina?			
Without ejaculation		4.3	4.5
Until ejaculation		5.6	—
With condom		4.3	—
Without condom		4.9	—
Removing the penis before ejaculation		3.1	—
Have you orally stimulated . . .			
A woman?		1.2	—
A man?		61.1	50.0
Have you been orally stimulated by . . .			
A woman?		3.7	4.5
A man?		76.5	95.5

Source: Jacobo Schifter and Johnny Madrigal, *Hombres que Aman Hombres,* San José, Costa Rica, ILEP-SIDA, 1992.

Chapter 9

The Lovers of Libano

To explain the upsurge of AIDS diagnoses among transvestites in recent years, one issue that warrants careful attention is the sort of love relationships in which these men engage. Quite simply, while acknowledging transvestites' versatility with their clients and their frequent use of condoms, in the past there has been considerable reticence among their lovers (a high proportion of whom were from San José's Libano district) to adopt safe sex practices themselves, which was confirmed when we interviewed several such individuals in 1990. The decreasing number of clients hailing from Libano over the past ten years is expected to have a positive effect on the incidence of safe sexual practices among transvestites. Nevertheless, there can be little doubt that their particular worldview has had an impact upon the AIDS epidemic in the past, and indeed continues to have one, given that there are still some Libano men among transvestites' roster of clients.

WHO ARE THEY?

The gender construction of the men who were the transvestites' lovers in the 1980s was strongly masculine. In our interviews with them, it was clear that, despite enjoying an intimate relationship with a transvestite, they identified closely with the "macho" style of gender and sexuality. Their lifestyle was similar to that of any other Costa Rican heterosexual male: married with children, attracted to stereotypically feminine qualities. They did not recall any childhood feelings of being either "different" or attracted to their own sex, as typically occurs with men who are gay. In the interviews, there was no evidence to suggest that they felt any attraction to men other than their transvestite lovers.

For the most part, the clients interviewed were blue-collar workers with very low incomes and little formal education. Juan Carlos sold Jell-O at a local market and made roughly 400 colones (U.S. $4) a day; he had formerly worked as a mechanic and shoemaker. Delio was an unemployed construction worker who had left school after the sixth grade. Pablo had worked as an accountant in a warehouse, but was currently out of work and had turned to petty theft. Louis worked as a salesclerk in a hardware shop and earned 3,600 colones (U.S. $36) per week. David had completed his second year of high school, and was currently employed as a butcher for roughly 5,000 colones (U.S. $50) per week.

At the time of the interviews, several of these men were being supported by their transvestite lovers. For example, Moses said that he was with Monique "for the money," while Pablo, who was financially dependent upon Paula, said that he felt uncomfortable with this arrangement and that he had also supported her in the past. All of Ricardo's living expenses were paid for out of Felicia's earnings and, in the case of Delio, he reported receiving some money from Corina because he was out of work.

This is not to say that all of the men interviewed were dependent upon their lovers for support. David, for example, used to give 1,000 colones to his transvestite partner, while Daniel and Miguel, who both lived with Rita, helped her out by handing over a portion of their wages.

The majority of the men interviewed made at least some use of drugs and/or alcohol. Pablo drank beer and consumed marijuana and cocaine, all the while living off Paula's earnings. Delio regularly spent 5,000 colones on beer, cocaine, and marijuana, even though he was unemployed. Juan Carlos drank beer and snorted cocaine, and spent roughly 500 colones a day on marijuana (despite the fact that he was only earning 400 colones per day). Indeed, only Felicia's partner, Ricardo, and Laura's boyfriend, Luis, stated that they did not consume any drugs at all, though Luis did admit that he engaged in regular bouts of binge drinking.

HETEROSEXUAL AND HOMOSEXUAL ACTIVITY

The life histories of the men who were the transvestites' lovers reveal that for the most part they had been unambiguously heterosexual prior to their involvement with a transvestite. Some, such as Luis, were married and had children. Miguel had had five heterosexual relationships before meeting Rita, while Daniel had also been with women prior to commencing a series of relationships with transvestites two years previously. David was twenty-nine years old and had been in a transvestite relationship for the past five years; before this, he had only had heterosexual encounters, with two children being their legacy. Finally, Moses, who was currently in a relationship with a transvestite, had had both male transvestite and female lovers in the past.

Despite prior heterosexual activity, all those interviewed said that they were very satisfied with their transvestite relationships and most, Delio and Louis excepted, no longer engaged in any sexual activity with women at all. When asked why this was the case, a similar reason was given by all: that greater pleasure was derived from a transvestite relationship, due to the fact that transvestites tended to be warmer, more passionate, sexier, and tighter than most women.

IN THE TRANSVESTITES' WORLD, THE PENIS DOES NOT MAKE THE MAN

Even though transvestites are men, as are their partners, it should be emphasized that transvestite culture differs markedly from that of the gay community in Costa Rica more generally. In large measure, this might be understood in terms of the highly particular meaning attributed to gender by transvestites and their lovers alike. In short, "femaleness" is subsumed under "femininity" in order to produce transvestites who are, as far as their clients and lovers are concerned, women, regardless of the fact that they happen to possess a male sexual organ.

Thus, for the male partner of a transvestite, his involvement with the latter is perceived in purely heterosexual terms: he is a man and his partner is a woman. At a more basic level, this is expressed in the assertion, often heard among the men interviewed, that he was the one who engaged in penetration during anal sex. Furthermore, this is also heard in many of the men's comments. For example, Paula's partner Pablo stressed that he is the "man in the relationship." Melvin said that he is so masculine that he does not even want to see the penis of his lover Lina. In this way, one might argue that unwillingness on the part of these men to acknowledge their lovers' sexual organs is closely related to their reticence to see themselves either as johns or as homosexual.

However, it should be noted that others stated that even though they were the active partner in anal sex, it did not bother them that their partner was endowed with a penis, with Ricardo even going so far as to say that he liked it because "it was different." Still, most denied ever having been penetrated themselves: Shasta's partner Jorge stated that "I play the role of the male and she the female"; Moses emphasized that it is he who "screws Monique," as did Juan Carlos. The only exception in this regard was Daniel, who admitted to having been penetrated by Rita.

SELF-DEFINITION AS CACHERO

Thus, it is clear that most of the interview participants defined their "manhood" in terms that did not differ significantly from heterosexual men more generally. Being a man entailed "screwing" women or other men. It is for precisely this reason that most of the men interviewed did not feel that they were gay and did not participate in any gay social activities. While some saw themselves as bisexual, others as either exclusively heterosexual or homosexual, most defined themselves as *cachero*. This is a word that can mean many things.

As noted above, Pablo saw himself as the man and Paula the woman; by no means did he consider himself a man who liked other men, even though he admitted to being bisexual. In similar fashion, Jorge defined himself as heterosexual, as did Moses, who used the word *buga* when talking about himself, Costa Rican slang for "straight." Significantly, Ricardo was the only man interviewed who considered himself homosexual; all the others saw themselves as *cachero*. Juan Carlos defined this term as an individual who has sex with homosexuals yet is not one himself. For Louis, it was a man who sleeps with both men and women; for David, it was "a man who screws queers." Finally, Delio and Miguel defined it as one who gives pleasure to others of the same sex, while Melvin suggested that it is a homosexual who acts like other men.

It was not only the partners of transvestites who did not consider themselves homosexual; the transvestites interviewed did not deem themselves gay either. This view is underscored by the fact that 91 percent of transvestites (compared with 13 percent of gay bar patrons) interviewed were in complete agreement with the statement, "it is better that one's lover be heterosexual"; another, smaller group, were somewhat in agreement with this statement. This in turn would explain not only why transvestites preferred to become involved with men who saw themselves as heterosexual rather than homosexual, but also why they did not feel they belonged to a group that was at high risk of HIV infection.[1]

PARTNERS' KNOWLEDGE OF AIDS

From the outset, it must be acknowledged that the transvestites' lovers were aware of the serious consequences associated with contracting AIDS. Juan Carlos knew that AIDS was a threat "because one is so close to the problem." Both Jorge and Moses were aware that HIV is transmitted through sexual contact and the exchange of bodily fluids, and that a condom is the only protection. Interestingly however, while both Luis and David also indicated that they knew of the dangers associated with HIV infection, they went on to stress that they themselves generally did not use condoms.

This is an important point, because it underlines the fact that although the transvestites' lovers are to some extent knowledgeable about HIV and AIDS, limited schooling and low income have conspired to deprive them of the tools needed to take preventative action. As the findings of Costa Rica's National AIDS Survey[2] suggest, it is precisely those who are poorly educated and poorly paid who are most averse to condom use. In the particular case of the transvestites' lovers, this reticence is aggravated in turn by the effects of drug addiction.

How so? As has already been suggested, the majority of partners were regular users of one or more drugs, and these drugs tended to be expensive, costing from 1,000 to 12,000 colones per week. The paucity of their own wages made them dependent upon their lovers, particularly if they were also attempting to support a second household or had children. When one combines financial dependence with frequent intoxication, the net effect is of course to place these individuals at high risk of contracting HIV, since they are not in a position to make an informed choice about safe sex and other high-risk activities.

In a further irony, they were also indirectly dependent upon their lovers' johns, since it was the latter's money that was used to support their drug habit. Needless to say, for men who subscribed to a "macho" understanding of masculinity, this led to feelings of jealousy and humiliation, feelings that were controlled and/or expressed in one of two ways:

A. Establishing alternative rules regarding jealousy and socialization: rather than jealousy being directed toward the clients, it tended to be focused on other *cacheros* or other transvestites. This often resulted in the breakdown of ties of solidarity.

Although the transvestites' lovers had to accept the fact that their partners were prostituting themselves, they would often experience jealousy. Pablo for example stated that he "feels bad" when Paula was with another man, even though he knew why she did it. Paula, on the other hand, would become jealous when Pablo spoke with other women. In another case, Ricardo admitted that "he is not jealous" of his partner, for, if he were, "she would not sell herself that way." He stated that he was not jealous of her because he knew that with others she did it for money, while with him it was for love. However, he did admit that Felicia was jealous of other transvestites. Unlike Pablo and Ricardo, Luis said that he was bothered by Laura's relationship with other men, as he felt that "she does it because she wants to."

Miguel and Daniel, who lived with Rita, were also bothered by their lover's work in the sex trade. Miguel recognized that he felt more jealousy than she did. Daniel disapproved of Rita's profession but felt that "there is nothing that we can do about it."

David was also aware that his lover prostituted herself and engaged in petty theft, but said that "Christina would not do it if I were there, and I also don't like it when she talks about what she did on the strip." Louis rationalized his partner's activities in a somewhat different fashion: he simply refused to visit the places where he knew Salomé worked. He also indicated that Salomé had tried to comfort him by saying that "it's the only thing I can do well" and that "it gives us money for our vices." Along somewhat similar lines, Delio also acknowledged that he was jealous of Corina, though not on account of her activities in the sex trade, but rather because of her relationships with other *cacheros*.

This is a significant finding, as it serves to underscore the fact that much of the lovers' jealousy is directed toward men such as themselves (i.e., lovers of other transvestites), thereby hindering the development of communication networks or a sense of group solidarity. In short, the men interviewed saw other *cacheros* principally as rivals, and thus friendships among them were extremely rare. Needless to say, this stands in marked contrast to the situation within the gay community, where the cultivation of close social relationships is the norm rather than the exception.

As one might imagine, the relative isolation of transvestites and their lovers from either the gay community or mainstream society has served not only to slow the spread of knowledge about safe sex, but it has also effectively prevented the development of community norms concerning the importance of taking HIV-prevention measures seriously. Because of this, transvestites were left dangerously exposed to the whims and prejudices of their clients and the *cacheros*, many of whom did not consider themselves to be part of a high-risk group.

B. Establishing alternative rules governing sexual relations with transvestites, in terms of behavior (being the active partner in anal sex) and practice (for example, engaging in sex without a condom in order to differentiate it from prostitution)

Among the partners interviewed, most preferred not to use a condom, even though they were aware that their lovers were engaged in the sex trade. In short, not only did the men tend to associate condom use with casual sex, but they felt as well that it diminished the level of physical pleasure. This of course stands in sharp contrast to the transvestites, who for the most part looked favorably upon the use of condoms. However, the fact that the latter generally deferred to their partners' wishes ensured that one was seldom used when they slept together.

Should one require confirmation of this finding, one need only turn to the individual responses themselves. Luis, for one, said that he did not use a condom because "If we're faithful it does not matter. It has been three years and we're still not seropositive." Shasta's partner Jorge expressed a similar view, stating that he did not like how it felt and that it was in any case unnecessary because he was "faithful." Others, such as Christina's lover David, refused to wear a condom because AIDS, as far as he was concerned, was "like any other venereal disease, like syphilis, gonorrhea, or cancer—one can catch it at any moment. We all have to die sometime; a lot of people who take care of themselves get sick sooner. I just don't like condoms." Interestingly, a number of the men interviewed, including Pablo and Moses, stressed that although they did not use a condom with their partners, they did wear one if they were engaging in sex with someone else. Indeed, only three partners, specifically Ricardo, Delio, and Louis, stated that they always used a condom, though Louis went on to admit that he does upon occasion forget to put one on when he is under the influence of drugs.

Thus, even as one acknowledges the degree to which such factors as socioeconomic marginalization and substance abuse are capable of rendering condom use unlikely, adequate attention must be paid as well to the condom's symbolic power. Quite simply, by associating sex for money with condom use, and sex for love with unsafe sex, an individual who felt powerless to stop his partner from prostituting herself was able to regain some sense of control in the relationship. As is suggested above, this is also seen in the assignment of roles during the sex act itself: by insisting that he be the one who penetrates the other during anal sex, the *cachero* is once again able to reassert his own sense of power and self-determination.

In this regard, it is important to recognize that the love expressed by the partner in his refusal to wear a condom is sincere. That is to say, despite the pressures associated with financial dependence and substance abuse, both transvestite and lover considered their relationship something very special, underpinned by feelings of love and tenderness.

This is apparent in the men's comments. Both Juan Carlos and Delio said that they loved their respective partners, with the latter stating that he wanted to be with Corina because she was "such a beautiful person." Along similar lines, Melvin indicated that he loved Lina and felt very hurt that his mother had rejected her, while Louis said that Salomé gave him everything he wanted and that he had already introduced her to his brother, who had accepted the relationship. David indicated that he loved Christina so much that he had his parents meet her and that, even though they knew she was a man, "They never said anything and they don't put her down, and once I took her to the house and they treated her well." Others expressed their feelings in similarly strong terms, with Pablo saying that he had kissed and hugged Paula in public, while Ricardo and Jorge insisted that their partner was preferable to any woman they had been with in the past.

These statements also serve to confirm the fact that *cacheros* are not afraid to take risks for the sake of their relationships. For example, some lived openly with their partners, while others were willing to be seen in public together, despite the physical and verbal harassment that this inevitably entails. The majority of the men interviewed admitted that it hurt when others made fun of their transvestite lovers, and that this had led to fights on more than one occasion. Still, it must be acknowledged that there were some who were considerably more reticent in this regard, though even here it was generally because they were afraid of losing their jobs.

Thus, in the final analysis, love manifested itself for both the transvestite and the *cachero* in the actions and risks that each was willing to take for the sake of their relationship. For them, AIDS was simply one of the risks that must be faced, since loving partners should not have to use condoms when engaging in sex. Needless to say, this in turn explains why so many in the transvestite community have come down with AIDS over the course of the past decade.

Chapter 10

The Sky Is the Limit

Electra is a Panamanian transvestite who makes heads turn. Her body is thin yet curvaceous, her face effeminate, her hair long, her voice high-pitched, and her manner delicate. Needless to say, she passes easily for a woman. "When I go to Key Largo [a San José bar known as a hangout for heterosexual prostitutes serving the city's expatriate and tourist communities], no one believes I'm a man," she said with pride. Her clients are as likely to be straight as bisexual: "Men pick me up who'd never dream of having an affair with a transvestite. I love the young American guys, who say it's like being in bed with a real woman."

When we asked Electra how she came to be in Costa Rica, she noted that it is easier to make money here if one is "svelte and good-looking like I am." She is one among dozens of transvestites who have come to work in the isthmus's new sexual mecca. "Here, people are more tolerant and respectful than they are in the other countries of the region," she says casually.

Panamanian transvestites are famous for being "perfect women," that is to say, for having faces and bodies that are so feminine in appearance that they are able to deceive even the most discerning among their clientele. Needless to say, Costa Rican transvestites consider them dangerous competitors. In Karla's words, the Panamanians' arrival "has been bad for us, because no one can compete with those bodies." It should be noted that Panamanians and other foreigners have brought with them something other than mere beauty and sensuality: they have introduced an alternative way of behaving in bed.

To illustrate, we quote Electra as she describes her "trauma" when she first slept with a Costa Rican client:

I'm used to johns who are "manly men." When I first came to San José I didn't know how things worked here. Well, I pick up my first client in the Biblica district, a tall, masculine-looking man who's quite handsome, the sort of guy I like. We go to a motel and agree on the rate. He starts kissing me passionately, and next thing I know he's got his hand on my genitals. "What's going on?" I yell, pissed off. "I'm a woman, dammit!" I tell him furiously. He didn't understand that I'm not the sort of transvestite who wants to have my organ touched. I didn't come here to sleep with men who are looking for cock. If that's what they're looking for, they should find themselves a fag. In Costa Rica, men who pick up transvestites want you to fuck them or else they want to blow you off. In my country, the men are real men. No real man would do what they're doing here.

Electra is not the only one who does not understand Costa Rican sexuality; Nicaraguan transvestites share her view. Esmeralda, for one, believes that the roles are more rigidly defined in her country. Being the active partner is acceptable; being the passive one is not. As she put it, "In Costa Rica the men who go cruising for transvestites are masculine in appearance, but they love it when you take them from behind."

Needless to say, this attitude has resulted in considerable conflict. Foreign transvestites will chide their clients for their "passivity," while seeking out men whom they consider more heterosexual in orientation. Although this may seem to be a contradiction in terms, in fact it is not. Electra, for example, now looks for clients in heterosexual locales, that is to say cabarets, bars, and other nightspots frequented by men who are seeking women. Of course, the incursion of transvestites into these locales has had a number of significant effects, not least of which is the engendering of a new client base:

I love going to Key Largo. I sit at a table with a few friends of mine who are hookers, and wait for someone to invite me for a drink. Last week, a man showed up who was very handsome and nothing less than the owner of a car rental agency. He started flirting with me and saying all these romantic things.

Before I could do anything, he kissed me on the lips. I really liked him because he was so young. The truth is I drank a lot that night, and so before I was even aware of it I had already got in his car. He took me to his apartment in La Sabana and we sat down in the living room to have another drink. That's when I told him that I was a transvestite. At first he was pissed off, and said that he was going to take me back to the bar. But, when I took off my top and he saw my tits, he took a drink and started kissing me again. He told me it was the first time he'd ever made love with a transvestite. I said that I understood that he might be feeling a bit nervous. Nervous my ass! We made love four times that night, and yesterday he called to ask me out again.

Although he may not be aware of it, the owner of the car rental agency is helping to give a new twist to the evolution of transvestism in Costa Rica. If he had not run into Electra in the bar that night, he probably never would have had a sexual liaison with another man, nor would the thought of having one even crossed his mind.

Thus, the fact that most of the johns who seek out transvestites are those who enjoy their versatility in bed has pushed a growing number of transvestites to venture into new pastures to find men who are "100 percent active," as Esmeralda would say. Indeed, Esmeralda herself has taken the step of visiting such popular heterosexual nightclubs as Infinito and Cocoloco in El Pueblo, a popular commercial district in San José. Men who would have never considered sleeping with a transvestite flirted with her. A few of them, such as the protagonist of the anecdote related above, go on to have an affair, in the process finding a new way of obtaining sexual fulfillment. In this way, bars that were exclusively heterosexual cease be so, while the world of transvestism acquires a few new devotees.

THE BASKETBALL PLAYER

Gustavo is both a basketball player and a businessman. He is doing very well financially ever since his company began to flourish and expand into the global market. His wife and two-year-old daughter are his pride and joy. Every time he wins a game, he dedicates his victory to them: "I love my family and I'm really proud of Yorleni, my little girl. She reminds me of myself, and she looks just like my wife."

Although Gustavo is widely known for his skill in basketball, there is one secret none of his fans are privy to: he is Miranda's brand-new lover, who is herself one of the most beautiful and sought-after transvestites in the country.

After several attempts, I convinced Miranda to arrange an interview with him on my behalf. "But why do you want to talk to him?" she asked me. "Well, I'm interested in meeting him and, besides, I'm a fan of his team," I answered. "Well, let's say you're a fan of his basketball team, darling, because nobody knows anything about the other team he plays for," she said jokingly. "I'll introduce you, but no photos, no descriptions, no hints even. I don't want you writing anything that might get him identified." I nodded: "No one will find out anything, I promise."

Two months later, Miranda invited me to her apartment, a nicely appointed condominium with three bedrooms, two baths, a patio, and a dining room. "Come in," she greeted me. "Make yourself at home." The transvestite was dressed in a black cotton outfit festooned with white satin epaulettes, and had a white orchid pinned to her breast and a string of pearls around her neck. "You're looking beautiful," I said sincerely as I walked past into her living room. There were two or three brown leather armchairs positioned around a coffee table of black glass. On the wall was a photo of Miranda, dressed in red with blonde hair streaming over her shoulders. "That's my own hair," she said. "Gustavo is taking a bath and he'll be with us in a moment. Can I bring you a drink?" The transvestite's life had certainly changed for the better over the course of the past six years. I remember seeing her through a dirty curtain in one of the old Libano bunkers. On an exquisitely carved cabinet were displayed some of her trophies. "Miss Peru Transvestite 1996," said one. Another, smaller one was engraved with the inscription, "Miss Gay Costa Rica," given to her by a local homosexual organization. "That one was given to me after a really bitter struggle. The president of the association didn't want me to get it and did everything in his power to make sure I lost," she recounted sadly. "Here, I've brought you a glass of white wine," she said, passing the glass to me as she sat down.

How's the book on transvestites going?

Well, good, but there's still quite a bit I have to do before I can finish it.

I admire you for being able to work with such nut cases. It must be difficult.

In fact, everybody's treated me well. How did Gustavo react to my request? Did it bother him?

It did at first. He can't let himself be found out. You know he's married with a little girl. His wife doesn't know anything about me, and she'd die if she found out. It's been hard on me because I love him so much. But I told him who you were and that it would help you a lot with the book. Besides, he admires your work. If he didn't, he never would've consented to the interview. He doesn't even let me invite my friends over when he's around. He just wants to make love and go home, that's it.

How did you meet him?

Nowhere less than Zapote, about a year ago. I was at this straight bar with Tina, another transvestite who's very feminine. At a table next to ours there were a number of players from the team. At first, I didn't pay any attention, even though I felt like I was being checked out from all sides. He's since told me that he didn't know I was a man at the time. I think it's true, because at first glance no one notices. In any case, while I was dancing with this other guy, he winked at me. Tina was the one who told me that he's a well-known basketball player. I know so little about the sport that she could've said he's a flying pig and it would have meant the same to me. Anyway, a little while later he asked me to dance. That night we exchanged telephone numbers and, the next weekend, he called me.

When did you tell him you were a man?

Only at the last possible moment. By that time he liked me so much that he couldn't let go of me. I played the difficult woman, I told him I didn't want any commitments, and I didn't want to go to bed right away. So it was three weeks before we actually made love.

And he never suspected anything?

I swear he didn't. He tells me now he did notice something strange about my voice, but at the time he didn't pay it any mind.

Is it difficult for you knowing that he's a married man?

Yes it is. I'd really like to go live with him, but I don't think it's going to happen. He's told me that he doesn't love his wife, that he married very young and that she's not that bright and doesn't understand him, but at the same time he's got a little girl who he loves very much.

How does he feel now that he knows you're really a man?

You can ask him yourself. The first few times we made love, he never touched me there. He didn't want to even know that I had a penis. But since then it's got easier. Even so, he's a man's man, I swear to you. He doesn't like it when I go at him from behind. He loves having women at his side. He's all stud!

A Man's Defiance

Gustavo entered the room. He's about twenty-seven years old, tall, handsome, and masculine. He greeted me casually, and then sat down next to Miranda, giving her a hug and a kiss as he did so. I couldn't help but be impressed: here was a man who is often seen on television, tenderly kissing his transvestite lover. Even if I told people what I had seen, I doubt many would believe me.

Gustavo, how do you think people would react if they found out about your relationship with Miranda?

You know what this country's like. I'd be crucified immediately. Some priest would come out of the woodwork all shocked and appalled, and I'd have a huge scandal on my hands. I can't afford that sort of luxury, and we're agreed that no information is going to come out of this, right?

Of course, and I want you to know that I appreciate your confidence in me. I won't use anything that would give people even the slightest hint of who you are. I'm only interested in writing generally about the sorts of relationships that transvestites are involved in. Are you happy with Miranda?

She knows that I love her greatly. For me, she's the ideal woman: feminine, cultured, delicate, and gracious. I never would've thought that I could feel this way about another man. However, I do want her to have the operation, because I'd really like her to be 100 percent woman. You know, with a body like that I think it's a shame she has a penis. Miranda is a real woman, it's just that she was born with the wrong genital organ.

How does she compare with your wife?

My wife's a country girl, simple. She's used to looking after the kid and having a man who tells her what to do. She's a good woman.

And how is she different from Miranda?

In everything. She's not as sensual, good-looking, and intelligent. Miranda is like a Hollywood actress. Besides, we're both very intense people. So when we're together there's an explosion. When we're making love, I feel like I've just scored in the world championship. This transvestite is able to make me feel something I've never felt with a woman. She knows exactly how to treat a man.

Do your friends suspect you're like this?

Like this, how?

Well, that you enjoy having a relationship with a transvestite.

Look, I've known various players and commentators who are gay. You can tell from how they look at you in the showers. A number of times I've noticed this guy or that guy checking out my penis. One time I even told this TV reporter, "look, it's my arm that scored that basket, not my dick. So would you mind looking somewhere else?" It never occurred to me to have an affair with another man. So why would anyone else suspect anything?

But you're famous. Aren't you worried that somebody might notice you coming into the building here?

Miranda knows very well how important it is right now that the relationship be kept very discreet. I give her all the happiness in the world, in a way that only a man can give, but I ask for discretion in return. When I come over, I enter quickly. Maybe at some point in the future, once she's had the operation and my girl's older, we'll get married. But for now we have to keep up appearances. I'm told that in other countries a few players live openly with transvestites, but not here in Costa Rica. It's not possible.

Miranda's Sorrow

Miranda seemed distant and sad. For the moment, in fin de siècle Costa Rica, a famous man cannot live openly with a transvestite. Still, I tried to console her: "Ten years ago, no transvestite here could have even dreamed of going with somebody like Gustavo. Given how quickly things are changing, don't you think that one day your relationship with him will be tolerated by society?" She looked at me sorrowfully and said, "By the time they let me get married in a church, I'll probably already have lost my teeth, my tits, and my ass. Can't you see that here people do whatever they want until it's time to lay their cards on the table, and then everybody just folds." "Well," I said, hoping to cheer her up, "maybe you'll just have to content yourself with being the team mother." "Oh, don't be ridiculous," she answered. "Their team already has one. She's somebody who works for a TV channel and she's always trying to interview them when they're showering, just so that she can pretend to make a mistake and grab their 'microphones,' all the while saying that it's only because she can't see too well."

However, despite the fact that Miranda cannot yet get married in a church, her relationship with Gustavo is indicative of a number of significant changes for the transvestite community. Not only are feminine transvestites such as Miranda able to mingle freely in heterosexual bars and nightclubs, but her lover is a far cry from those who call the Libano district home. Gustavo is in no way different from any of Miranda's neighbors in La Sabana; he is not poor, dependent, or a drug abuser. Moreover, he would never dream of engaging in sexual intercourse without using a condom. As he put it, "I use a condom with every woman I sleep with. Sometimes I go to El Pueblo to pick somebody up, but you can't trust any of those women. Really, a condom is indispensable for men like me."

INCONSISTENT CONDOM USE

Still, there are other young lovers of transvestites who, despite sharing Gustavo's class background, are not as conscientious as he is. In particular, there are now cases of wealthy transvestites who have "bought" themselves attractive men, by means either of drugs or money. Although these men may be gay, straight, or bisexual in orientation, the common thread unifying them is their involvement with transvestites in return for money, drugs, or pleasure. However, these men differ from those of the Libano in that they are more conscious of the dangers posed by AIDS, and hence are more likely to protect themselves, particularly in light of the fact that they are aware of their lovers' profession. However, it is also true that they do occasionally have intimate relations with women and other men where safe sex is not practiced:

> I know I should use a condom. But the other night I was at an orgy with Esther and one of her clients. I used a condom to make love to this guy twice while he was kissing Esther. But when it came to making love with her, I had run out of condoms. I'd already used the two I brought with me, and I didn't bring any for the john. So we made a deal: I told him that I'd make love to Esther while he watched, but that he couldn't have her himself without a condom. He then said that he'd pay more if I let him make love to her. I thought about it but said no, it's a show or nothing, and anyway it was his own fault for being so horny and not having enough condoms. It was a big enough risk that me and Esther were taking making love without a condom.

In another case, Alberto, the bisexual lover of a transvestite, often forgets to practice safe sex when intoxicated:

I can't swear to you that I always use a condom. There are times I'm so fucked up that I even forget my own name. Like the other day I went out with Tere, and we were in a motel room smoking some joints laced with coke. I suggested we have a bath together and soap ourselves down. So I brought my beer with me and we had our bath. Afterward, all I can remember is Tere taking the cell phone and calling her lover. It seemed they were fighting and I thought I'd stir things up a bit. So I took the phone and told him exactly what we were doing, including the sizes and positions and everything. The guy started insulting me and threatening to kill me. That brought out the sadist in me, and so I went into the other room and started saying stuff to Tere just so he'd hear. Then I took the phone and told him all the things I was gonna do to her. I told him how I'd already undressed her and soaped her down, and how I was going to screw her like nobody had ever screwed her before. I also told him that she'd said that mine's much bigger than his and how she liked me a lot more than him. All I could hear on the other end of the line was him weeping with rage. Finally, I told him that it was my line and that it was gonna be an expensive call, and then I hung up on him. Now how am I supposed to remember to use a condom when all this shit's going down?

TAXI! TAXI!

"When we were poor and destitute," recounted Esmeralda, "we had a very special relationship with taxi drivers." According to her, in the era of the Libano cinema, transvestites did not use taxis very often. "But we always had an understanding with them, since transvestites, when they're going on a visit, they have to take a cab because bus drivers either won't let them on, or else they'll make life impossible for them. But the relationship has gotten even more intense since we moved to the Clinica Biblica district."

Curious about this relationship, I asked Esmeralda about it in more detail:

So, you would say that transvestites and taxi drivers have a special bond?

Of course! We're among taxi drivers' best clients. We use them a lot to get to motels or other places where we can make love. Not so much before, because in the Libano brothels everything happened in the same place. But now that we're on the street, we use them to go to and from the area where all the motels are. You just tell them when you want them to come back to pick you up and they will. It's a good arrangement.

Are a lot of them homophobic?

There's one or two who'll go on about the Bible and this sort of stuff, but most of them are in it for the money. Besides, they're used to taking people to motels, and some even make a business out of supplying them with prostitutes. In any case, they're cool with us. If there's a raid or something, they'll even hide us and protect us from the cops, since after all we are their best customers.

And what about this business of relationships?

Oh, my dear, that's common knowledge! Last week I was heading home at about three in the morning. I stopped a cab and asked him to take me to González Lahmann [a neighborhood in San José]. I got in and started talking with him. He told me what a long day he was having, how he'd been taking people to motels for the last three hours. I noticed that he was a young guy, about twenty-four. He asked how things had gone for me that night. "Only two tricks the whole night," I answered. He looked at me through his rearview mirror and said, "What a shame! And you're so pretty." I pretended I didn't hear anything, just continued talking, and then he said, "Why don't you come up here, darling, and I won't charge you anything?" I moved up to the front seat and said, "Look, I'm worth much more than a little ride in your taxi. I'm coming up 'cause I like you." He drove us up to Zurqui and, when we got there, we made love. I got home at around six.

Other transvestites corroborated Esmeralda's statement, arguing that emotional and sexual ties between taxi drivers and transvestites are quite common. As Laura explained, "It's one group that's very supportive of us because we use their services so much."

Indeed, among San José's male heterosexual population, there are few who benefit more from the transvestite sex trade than taxi drivers. Pana, for example, is often asked to supply gay hotels with transvestites. "Pedro, it's Pana! Can you bring us a young, feminine-looking transvestite for a group of gringos who are staying at the hotel?" says a voice on his cellular phone. "The only ones on the corner right now are Dolores and Lola," he answers. "Go see if you can find Marilyn, she's probably the youngest one around." "Listen, bud, how much are talking about here?" Pedro asks. "We told the gringos two hundred dollars for two hours, but that's for all three of them." "I'll see what I can do," the driver answers. Eduardo not only supplies hotels with prostitutes, but he even provides a mobile motel service of his own. "Lots of transvestites will simply do their business back there while I drive. It's very safe because I'm here and everybody knows I'm watching. I charge for the ride plus two thousand colones. If there's intercourse, I charge three thousand to cover damage to the seat." Louis has benefited from the sex trade both financially and personally:

> At first it was strictly business with Leslie. I took her to the motels and nothing more, though I won't say I didn't notice her 'cause she's very pretty. Anyway, one time I picked her and a john up and took them to Zurqui. Anyway, the guy couldn't get off, and since he wasn't satisfied, he didn't want to pay. As for myself, I took Leslie's side because I'd already lost more than an hour and anyway she deserved to get paid. Since the guy was such an asshole, it ended up coming to blows. He started punching Leslie in the face, until I finally walloped him and threw him out of the car onto the highway. Tears were streaming down Leslie's face, she was so mad. I took her out for a drink in Heredia and I enjoyed myself so much we ended up eventually in a motel by the Virilla river. It was since then that we became a couple.

Mario, although he has never become quite so involved with transvestites, has certainly grown to like them:

I've never thought about sleeping with a transvestite, they just don't turn me on. But I like them. They make me laugh, they have a good sense of humor. One night I picked up Lulu with this old gringo whose jaw kept twitching. I'm sure he had some sort of nervous condition. Anyway, she asked me to take them to a motel, and then she said, "Do you think this gringo's got his jaw problem from giving too many blow jobs, or is it just because he's got a mouth full of ants?" I just can't believe some of the crazy things they say—like this other time Lulu was asking me how much she owed me, and when I told her she said, "Listen, why don't I just give your motor an oil change instead?" I laughed and I laughed, and finally I said, "You fiend! When you're finished with this guy, we'll talk!"

Significantly, some taxi drivers have even come to identify with the transvestites and the persecution they face. As one driver put it, "I used to be the first to say that we should kill all the queers. Now, after getting to know a few of them, I've changed my outlook, and I get pissed off when I see those sons of bitches coming to give them a hard time. I've gotten into a fight with more than one of them, I can tell you. When you get to know somebody, you can't keep hating him for no reason."

YET ANOTHER COMBINATION

As it happens, heterosexual men are not the only population to have recently fallen into the transvestites' web. Increasingly, they are being joined by another, even more unexpected group: heterosexual women. "What's this?" I exclaimed in surprise when Esmeralda told me this. "It's true, the last few tricks I've turned have been women, and I slept with them," she replied, without batting an eye. "How could this be? Tell me a bit more," I said, as I grappled with my incredulity.

There's nothing to explain. A couple weeks ago, for example, I was picked up by a couple. The man wanted to have the experience of being with a transvestite and a woman at the same time, while his girlfriend wanted to find out what transvestites looked like, how they did it, what they were like in bed. So anyway, we went to a motel and made love.

You had relations with both of them?

Of course. First the man made love to the woman, then he made love to me and then, finally, I made love to her. It was all very erotic.

What else happened?

Nothing too out of the ordinary. The woman and I talked about building one's bust, and how it was that I looked so shapely. I taught her a few tricks, like wearing ten panties one on top of the other to make one's hips seem bigger and one's waist smaller. Afterward we talked about men: what we liked them to do, how they are, that sort of thing.

What was he doing while this was going on?

He was just sitting there listening. He told me that this was the first time that he'd ever been with a transvestite, and that he'd really liked watching me make love to his girlfriend. He also asked her how it felt, and whether it was very different when I made love with her as compared to him. She said that it was different, but that she preferred him because I wasn't used to a woman's body and so didn't really know how to stimulate her.

How did you feel making love to her?

It's hard to explain. Here I was, a transvestite, making love to another woman. Is that lesbian or what? Myself, I'm not really into women, and I don't know anything about them. But because I knew the guy was watching me and he was getting turned on, that was turning me on too. Then, when I came, I looked the guy in the eyes, and at that moment it seemed like it was the two of us making love, indirectly.

But the truth is that you're a male and you were with a female. So weren't you playing the part of the straight man having sex with a woman?

No, no way! I'm telling you that I was dressed as a woman. My attitude was feminine, not aggressive. The man, meanwhile, was screwing both of us with his eyes. We did what he wanted us to do, he was in charge, it was a relationship between the two of us, and him.

But you screwed his girlfriend like you were a man yourself.

Yeah, but it doesn't matter who was screwing who, 'cause we were both under the thumb of the man.

Would you change this?

Well, all I can say is that on this occasion this guy had us both under his control. However, last week the same woman came back herself.

What for?

Well, she came to pick me up. She asked if I'd get in the car with her, and I thought to myself, money is money, and got in.

So off you two went.

To the same hotel in fact, this time by ourselves. She told me that she'd broken up with the guy because he's such a womanizer. He had even slept with her own sister in their house. I thought she wanted to be comforted, so I said, "don't you cry. Men are just a bunch of liars really, they're just not worth the trouble." She was sitting there with tears running down her face, but it seemed like she wanted something else as well.

What made you think that?

She took my hand and put it on her breast and said to me, "I've always had this fantasy of going to bed with an old friend of mine who would then take me as though she was a man." I told her that there was no way I'd be able to satisfy her, because in the first place I wasn't this old friend of hers, and I wasn't into women anyway. Maybe she should go looking for a lesbian instead. "No," she said. "I don't like lesbians! I want to be with someone who's intimate like a woman, but built like a man so that I can have orgasms." She asked me if I'd help her and said that she'd pay ten thousand for sex. She even laid the money down on the bed. "Okay," I said. "But we're going to do this step by step. First, we'll kiss and caress each other while you're dressed as a woman. Then, you'll go to the bathroom and take off all your makeup and clothes, and then come back to the bed. I've brought makeup so you can do yourself up afterward."

And then what happened?

At first I wasn't really into it, but it got better once I started imagining that we were two lesbians going at it, and that her husband was going to catch us and then it would be the three of us together. As I kissed her I started feeling a little horny. I then went into the bathroom to wash myself and take off some of the clothes I was wearing. Afterward, I went back into the bedroom and made love to her. At that moment, I was feeling more mannish. She told me that she loved being with me and how she had lied before, that I was a better lover than her old boyfriend, and that I knew how to turn her on. And that's about the end of it.

Did you think that someday you'd end up in bed with a woman?

It never crossed my mind. If the situation had been different, if I hadn't been offered the money, I wouldn't have done it. I don't like women.

Esmeralda is not the only one who has had this experience. Other transvestites have indicated that they too have been involved in ménages à trois or larger groups in which there have been an equal number of men and women. Once in the motel room, the interactions are often complex. In some cases, the women like to watch their men have sex and others enjoy participating themselves, while the more daring will even use dildos, cucumbers, or sausages to penetrate the transvestites present. Some johns do not want their women to have sex with the transvestites, while others do not mind. On some occasions, the men will engage in relations with other men, while the women will become intimate with other women. In moments such as these, future trysts are often arranged. To cite Pepa, "This one time I was in bed with two women while the men went out to get a drink and bring us back some snacks, and one of the women told me that she'd like to have another fling with me the following week, same time, same place."

NOT EVEN LESBIANS ESCAPE

There are also cases where women turn up alone, without any men present at all. I asked Artemis to describe one such encounter:

The latest thing is for lesbians or single women to come down to the strip.

Tell me about this.

Last night, for example, I was approached by two women. They were lesbians. One was very mannish and the other more feminine. They offered me eight thousand colones to put on a little show for them in their apartment. Afterward, the mannish one told me to undress and to start kissing her girlfriend, while she'd pretend to suddenly come home and discover us making love. So we started touching and stuff, while she locked herself in the bathroom. About five minutes later she came out dressed all in leather, with a black hat and boots and a whip. She hit me a few times with it, and the girlfriend as well. Not very hard mind you, but it still hurt a bit. Then, she pulled out a dildo and took me from behind.

What are these women looking for in transvestites? A sensible man, for a start. For straight women, transvestites are a sort of middle ground between heterosexuality and lesbianism. When they are with one, they do not feel that they themselves have become lesbian. Moreover, they are with a man who has not rejected his feminine side. As several clients put it, transvestites are "sweeter, more sensible and caring, and have a better sense of humor" than other, more "masculine" men. Thus, the women can become more intimate with transvestites than is possible with their usual sex partners. Along similar lines, transvestites can appreciate—and discuss—issues such as women's clothing and makeup.

Others by contrast seek out transvestites to obtain the sexuality of a man in the shape of a woman. Lesbians in particular, some of whom are faced with sexual identity problems, are often drawn to the type of intimacy transvestites offer. Given that the latter are women with the souls and sexuality of men, these lesbians feel that they are able to experiment more openly with alternative forms of sexuality. Of course, it is for a similar reason that many heterosexual men are attracted to "phallic" women. Many of the latter say that they particularly like transvestites' aggressiveness.

Thus, for the reasons outlined above, transvestites now have relations with individuals drawn from both genders and all sexual orientations. If they fail to use a condom, as has sometimes been known to happen, they can transmit or receive HIV (and hence AIDS) from any segment of the population. To quote Marilyn, "The sky is the limit. There's now no sector of society that's free of the webs we've spun."

Conclusion

One of the objectives of this study was to ascertain the degree to which transvestites employed in the sex trade are at risk of becoming infected with HIV. Another more general aim was to enhance our understanding of transvestites' sexual culture, along with the dreams and problems they face on a day-to-day basis. During the course of the work, we have seen how low self-esteem, societal discrimination, lovers' attitudes, substance use, and the particular pressures exerted by lovers and johns are all factors in inducing transvestites to practice unsafe sex upon occasion.

We have also learned that prostitution is the only career avenue open to men who feel a need to dress as women. If discrimination did not exist in Costa Rica, it is clear that this would not be their only profession. Another objective of this research was to examine how a simple relocation in space, associated with the phenomenon of *paqueteo*, could produce such deep-seated changes in the lives of transvestites and their clients. Not only has this relocation resulted in different social classes becoming involved in the sex trade as johns or in practicing transvestism themselves, but it has also led individuals to experiment with alternative forms of sexual practice, whether these be genital, emotional, or imaginary in scope.

Contrary to the essentialist position, this book has provided evidence in support of a more elastic view of human sexuality, whereby individuals' sexual orientation can undergo significant alteration completely independently of such factors as size of the hypothalamus, genetic background, or rates of hormone production.

In short, while the roots of contemporary transvestism in Costa Rica can be traced to the activities of marginalized strata of the population in the area around the Libano cinema, relocation by some of these transvestites to the Clinica Biblica district brought them in contact with a new, mostly middle-class clientele. As demand increased among the latter, the higher rates charged induced more and more middle-class adolescents to join the transvestite sex trade themselves as prostitutes.

Significantly, it was the arrival on the scene of these well-educated, relatively affluent transvestites that provided the basis for a number of legal battles in which members of the transvestite community defended their rights in court. Thanks to these actions an end was finally put to the arbitrary police roundups of the past.

In this way, not only were transvestites able to enlarge the areas given over to the sex trade, garnering new types of client in the process (such as heterosexual men and women), but San José's relatively tolerant atmosphere served to attract transvestites from elsewhere in Central America and the Caribbean basin, whose *paqueteo* abilities allowed them to penetrate hitherto forbidden heterosexual locales.

IS TRANSVESTISM REVOLUTIONARY?

If we were able to locate the source of individuals' sexual orientation, as some essentialist studies pretend to have done, would we be able to create a more just and rights-conscious society through the elimination of homosexuality, transvestism, and other sexual practices labeled "deviant"? I think not.

To the extent that we applaud diversity and celebrate difference, that we prefer innovation over stagnation, that we welcome the free play of divergent beliefs and thought, and that we are intrigued by different cultures and different ways of doing things, we owe it to ourselves to rejoice and welcome the recent transvestite revolution. Given the degree to which Costa Rica's underdevelopment might be explained in terms of the mental straitjacket that champions conventional wisdom at the expense of creative thought, it is clear that the presence of the transvestite community has benefited this country by forcing us to open our minds and reexamine our prejudices.

What is the harm—whether moral, spiritual, political, or ecological—in a man dressing himself in women's clothes? In a world full of misery, envy, war, hate, and corruption, what should it matter that a man likes to put on lipstick? Perhaps it is questions such as these that the masters of the media and keepers of the country's virtue would like us to consider, rather than addressing in their place the real moral failings of the present age: public institutions' contempt for the needs of the people; legalized extortion by the state from those who can least afford it; the hijacking of the country's electoral system by the traditional parties; the arrogance and hypocrisy of organized religion; the ecological and demographic disasters to which even now we are contributing; the erosion of solidaristic values; and many other capital crimes besides.

It is because of our discrimination and bigotry that transvestites have been forced to turn to drugs and prostitution. If we allowed them to go to work in our offices and stores dressed as women, there would not be hundreds of them standing on street corners at night. Of course, this is not to say that changes are not necessary within their own community. The struggle cannot be limited simply to the creation of a five-block tolerance zone for all of the country's transvestites. Instead, they must orient themselves to a larger project, one which will serve to open all those doors and opportunities that are now closed to them. It is only when a transvestite can work as a construction worker, executive secretary, member of congress or president that our work will be truly done. For this to occur, they will have to leave the street and the drugs behind. Prostitution should not be the only profession open to them; they must be able to fulfil their potential in any line of work they choose.

ILPES is currently involved in a program whose aim is precisely to sell transvestite cultural shows to hotels and restaurants serving the European and North American tourist markets. In another case, ILPES is endeavoring to develop a series of cooperative enterprises in the area of clothes manufacturing and hair styling. However, to become involved in these initiatives transvestites are asked to stop using drugs. In this way, the fight for equality must go hand in hand with the struggle to improve transvestites' public image.

A TRANSVESTITE PRESIDENT

To show that she means business, Anna Karenina presented to us the speech that she intends to read when she is elected president of Costa Rica:

Ladies and gentlemen, gentlemen dressed as ladies and ladies dressed as gentlemen:

When I was little, I never dreamed that I would one day
become president of Costa Rica. Those were hard times for
transvestites, when we were seen as a scourge of society. I still
remember the shame my father felt when he first saw me
dressed in girls' clothes, and the beating he gave me! Nor do I
forget the way the priests condemned us and incited the mob. I
have also not forgotten the many brave transvestites who were
killed at a tender age by homophobia and discrimination. May
God bless them and keep them, and my words do justice to
their sacrifice.

In the final years of the twentieth century Costa Ricans
experienced a great political change. After having put our trust
in men, we realized that all they did was steal from us. There
was not a single political institution that was free of corruption. Not only were men crooks and robbers, but they held
women in lower esteem than a dog's belly. Domestic violence,
incest, abuse, and sexual harassment were the order of the day.
It was thus thanks to the valiant women, supported by various
minority groups, that the revolution of 1998 was brought to a
successful close, fifty years after the previous one.

The fight was long and cruel. There were moments when
morale was low and we thought that we would lose the war.
Many of us went up to the front line to help entertain the
troops. We took many risks and some of us died for the moth-
erland. Not in battle, mind you, but after being electrocuted by
the poor quality light and sound equipment we were using.
The fallen were buried as heroines. One of the best known is
comrade Lulu, who encouraged the Liberation Army during
the final battle for San José. Lulu was crushed when one of her
heels gave way and she fell in the path of an armored car.
Meanwhile, Naranjita choked to death when she took fright
during a bombing raid and swallowed a sausage by mistake.

Once San José was liberated, the women proclaimed the
birth of a truly democratic republic, in which people could rise
to prominence regardless of their sex. Moreover, each candi-
date for high office was required to dress up in both men and

women's clothes in order to gain a sense of what it means to belong to each gender. The transvestites, because this is something we've always done, were declared the country's first citizens.

I promise you that I will adhere to the pacifist traditions that have made Costa Rica an example to the world, and a developed country in more recent years. Many of my friends have played a role in transforming our homeland. La Chepa, for example, revolutionized agricultural production by genetically engineering cucumbers, yuccas, and other tubers so that they might grow to a super-big size, generating considerable economic gains in the process. Eveltina invented a special computer program for transvestites in which every Windows workspace would be decorated with an attractive array of flowers and garlands. Pepa revolutionized LACSA's frequent-flyer program so that the johns from the Clinica Biblica would be given five hundred miles for each trick. Since then, the airline has never flown with an empty seat. Karla increased banana exports by raffling weekend getaway trips in gay bars. Marilyn transformed Punta Arenas into a new movie mecca by opening her liposuction clinic there and changing all the sex-trade workers into stunning models. Lola patented a new weapon that provided the basis for the country's nascent armaments industry: the jocote (seed from a tropical fruit that is thrown like a stone by children). Her use of the device to get rid of the rednecks who came to harass her in the Biblica proved to be a highly effective means of mob control.

I pledge myself to build upon this fine work. We transvestites have been the ones who have managed to place this country at the forefront of global development. We have taught all Costa Ricans the values that differentiate us from others in the region: tolerance, mutual respect, creativity, and ingenuity. Costa Rica, thanks to our efforts, has become known around the world as a paradise of human rights, ecological sensitivity, and sustainable development. Tourism has increased and so have our wages. Everyone wants to come visit the country that has achieved so much in the area of human rights. The arts and sciences have flourished.

Once the last vestiges of machismo were eliminated, our society underwent a cultural revolution. The country became the new artistic center of Latin America. Having rid ourselves of religious censorship, we were able to exploit our innate gifts to their full potential. Moreover, we were able to bring population growth under control thanks to family planning. This last achievement is in no small part due to the work of another comrade, Vaselina, who pushed condoms on every street corner. In one fell swoop, we eliminated poverty, unemployment, and illiteracy. Sex ceased to be seen as a sin and people learned to enjoy it without remorse or guilt. Not seeing it as something dirty anymore, we were able to delight ourselves in it just like we do in fine food, and were able to live without sexologists and psychologists.

I promise to carry on with this struggle while becoming president and first lady at the same time, something that will save us millions as well as solving a few problems. I will continue with the venerable tradition of my predecessors to give blow jobs at the president's Oral Office. I will of course charge for it and donate all proceeds to the AIDS Foundation. Finally, during my term in office I will spearhead the complete refurbishment of our horrible capital. Instead of depending on the bad taste of the political dinosaurs, I will form a committee drawn exclusively from the ranks of the transvestite community who will design, paint, and put in plants. The Clinica Biblica district will be named a national heritage site for being the place where the transvestite liberation movement was born. The neighbors who wanted us out so badly will be able to sell their houses to the State as national treasures.

Thank you very much.

Anna Karenina, President of Costa Rica

Notes

Introduction

1. *Paqueteo,* in the street language of transvestites, refers to the act of deceiving, of pretending, of feigning, in short of transforming oneself into something else. In this world, a transvestite who is successful in *paqueteo* is one who is able to pass for a woman.

2. Sigmund Freud, "Three essays on the theory of sexuality," *Standard Edition,* Vol. 7, London, Hogarth Press, 1953.

3. Sendor Ferenczi, "Nosology of homosexuality in men" in *Homosexuality in Modern Society,* ed. Heindrick M. Ruitenbek, Buenos Aires, Siglo XXI Publishers, 1973, p. 19.

4. Irving Bieber, Harvey S. Dain, Paul R. Dince, Marvin G. Drellich, Henry S. Grand, Ralph H. Gundlach, Malvina W. Kremer, Alfred H. Rifkin, Cornelia B. Wilbur, and Toby B. Bieber, *Homosexuality: A Psychoanalytic Study,* New York, Basic Books, 1962.

5. Evelyn Hooker, "Adaption of the manifestly homosexual" in *Homosexuality in Modern Society,* ed. Heindrick M. Ruitenbek, Buenos Aires, Siglo XXI Publishers, 1973, pp. 181-204.

6. Allen P. Bell, Martin S. Weinberg, and Sue Kiefer Hammersmith, *Sexual Preference: Its Development in Men and Women,* Bloomington, IN, Indiana University Press, 1981.

7. Ronald Bayer, *Homosexuality and American Psychiatry,* New York, Basic Books, 1981.

8. G. Dörner, W. Rohde, F. Stahl, L. Krell, and W. G. Masius, "A neuroendocrine predisposition for homosexuality in men," *Archives of Sexual Behavior,* 4, 1975, 1-8.

9. D. F. Swaab and M. A. Hofman, "An enlarged suprachiasmatic nucleus in homosexual men," *Brain Research,* 537, 1990, 141-148.

10. S. LeVay, "A difference in hypothalamic structure between heterosexual and homosexual men," *Science,* 257, 1991, 620-621.

11. L. S. Allen and R. A. Gorski, "Sexual orientation and the size of the anterior commissure in the human brain," *Proceedings of the National Academy of Science,* 89, 1992, 7199-7202.

12. E. O. Wilson, *Sociology: The New Synthesis,* Cambridge, MA, Belknap, 1975.

13. D. H. Hamer, S. Hu, V. L. Magnuson, N. Hu, and A. M. L. Pattatucci, "A linkage between DNA markers on the X chromosome and the male sexual orienta-

tion," *Science*, 261, 1993, 321-327. See also Dean Hamer and Peter Copeland, *The Science of Desire, the Search for the Gay Gene and the Biology of Behaviour*, New York, Simon and Schuster, 1994.

14. John P. De Cecco, "Definition and meaning of sexual orientation" in *Nature and Causes of Homosexuality: A Philosophical and Scientific Inquiry*, ed. Noreta Koertge, Binghamton, NY, The Haworth Press, 1983, pp. 51-86.

15. Vern L. Bullough and Bonnie Bullough, *Cross Dressing, Sex and Gender*, Philadelphia, University of Pennsylvania Press, 1993.

16. Walter C. Williams, *The Spirit and the Flesh: Sexual Diversity in American Indian Culture*, Boston, Beacon Press, 1986.

17. Sudhir Kakar, *The Inner World: A Psychoanalytic Study of Childhood and Society in India*, Oxford University Press, Oxford, UK, 1981.

18. N. Besnier, "Polynesian gender liminality through time and space" in *Third Sex, Third Gender: Beyond Sexual Disphormism in Culture and History*, ed. G. Herdt, New York, Zone Books, 1994, pp. 285-328.

19. J. Wellright, *Amazons and Military Maids: Women Who Dressed as Men in Pursuit of Life, Liberty and Happiness*, London, Pandora Press, 1989.

20. E. L. Meyer, "The soldier left a portrait and her eyewitness account," *Smithsonian*, 24 (10), 1994, 96-104.

21. Clement Wood, *The Woman Who Was Pope*, New York, William Faro, 1931.

22. R. J. Dekker and L. C. van de Pol, *The Tradition of Female Transvestism in Early Modern Europe*, New York, St. Martin's Press, 1989.

23. R. Judd, *Origins of Cross-Dressing: A History of Performance en Transvesti*, doctoral dissertation, Clayton University, 1988.

24. P. Ackroyd, *Dressing Up. Transvestism and Drag: The History of an Obsession*, New York, Simon and Schuster, 1979.

25. Didier Eribon, *Michel Foucault*, Barcelona, Anagrama, 1992, p. 25.

26. Deborah Heller Feinbloom, *Transvestites and Transsexuals: Mixed Views*, New York, Delta Books, 1977, p. 106.

27. Ibid., p. 106.

28. Ibid., p. 57.

29. John Money and Ehrhardt Anke A. *Man and Woman, Boy and Girl: Differentiation and Dimorphism of Gender Identity from Conception to Maturity*, Baltimore, John Hopkins University Press, 1978.

30. Jacobo Schifter and Johnny Madrigal, *Psychiatry and Homophobia*, San José, Editorial ILPES, 1997.

31. Robert Stoller, *Sex and Gender*, New York, Science House, 1968.

32. Allan P. Bell, Martin S. Weinberg, and Sue Kiefer Hammersmith, *Sexual Preference: Its Development in Men and Women*, Bloomington, IN, Indiana University Press, 1981.

Chapter 1

1. Frederick Witham and Robin Mathy, *Male Homosexuality in Four Societies: Brazil, Guatemala, the Philippines, and the United States*, New York, Praeger Scientific, 1986.

Chapter 2

1. Laura Chacon, Ana Lucia Gutierrez, Martiza Ortiz, Ana Rodriguez, and Alicia Zamora, "Jugar a ser mujer en cuerpo masculino: Un análisis sobre la prostitución travesti, prevención y sida," San José, University of Costa Rica, 1994.

2. Jacobo Schifter and Johnny Madrigal, *Ojos Que No Ven: Psiquiatría y Homofobia*, Editorial ILPES, San José, 1997.

3. Bonnie Bullough, Vern Bullough, and James Elias, *Gender Blending*, New York, Prometheus Books, 1997.

Chapter 3

1. A Costa Rican tabloid.
2. A Costa Rican painter.
3. A lower-middle-class neighborhood.

Chapter 4

1. An expression used to describe individuals who blush easily.
2. An extreme right political group with a paramilitary background.

Chapter 6

1. In 1997, an American dollar was worth approximately 245 colones.

2. Jacobo Schifter, *Lila's House: Male Prostitution in Latin America*, Binghamton, NY: The Haworth Press, 1998.

Chapter 7

1. INISA is the National Institute for Health Investigation, an official body that carries out HIV tests and offers treatment to those who are infected with the virus.

2. Jacobo Schifter and Johnny Madrigal, *Hombres que Aman Hombres*, San José, Costa Rica, ILEP-SIDA, 1992.

Chapter 8

1. Jacobo Schifter and Johnny Madrigal, *Hombres que Aman Hombres*, San José, Costa Rica, IMEDIEX, 1992.

2. Ibid.

3. R. A. Hatcher and M. S. Hughes, "The truth about condoms," *Siecus Report* 17 (2), November-December 1988, 1-9.

Chapter 9

1. Jacobo Schifter and Johnny Madrigal, *Hombres que Aman Hombres*, San José, Costa Rica, ILEP-SIDA, 1992.

2. Johnny Madrigal and Jacobo Schifter, *Primera Encuesta Nacional de SIDA*, San José, Costa Rica, ADC, 1990.

Index

Page numbers followed by the letter "t" indicate tables.

Order Your Own Copy of
This Important Book for Your Personal Library!

FROM TOADS TO QUEENS
Transvestism in a Latin American Setting

_____in hardbound at $39.95 (ISBN: 0-7890-0649-9)

_____in softbound at $14.95 (ISBN: 1-56023-958-1)

COST OF BOOKS_____

OUTSIDE USA/CANADA/
MEXICO: ADD 20% _____

POSTAGE & HANDLING_____
(US: $3.00 for first book & $1.25
for each additional book)
Outside US: $4.75 for first book
& $1.75 for each additional book)

SUBTOTAL_____

IN CANADA: ADD 7% GST _____

STATE TAX_____
(NY, OH & MN residents, please
add appropriate local sales tax)

FINAL TOTAL_____
(If paying in Canadian funds,
convert using the current
exchange rate. UNESCO
coupons welcome.)

☐ **BILL ME LATER:** ($5 service charge will be added)
(Bill-me option is good on US/Canada/Mexico orders only;
not good to jobbers, wholesalers, or subscription agencies.)

☐ Check here if billing address is different from
shipping address and attach purchase order and
billing address information.

Signature_____

☐ **PAYMENT ENCLOSED: $**_____

☐ **PLEASE CHARGE TO MY CREDIT CARD.**

☐ Visa   ☐ MasterCard   ☐ AmEx   ☐ Discover
☐ Diner's Club

Account # _____

Exp. Date _____

Signature _____

Prices in US dollars and subject to change without notice.

NAME _____

INSTITUTION _____

ADDRESS _____

CITY _____

STATE/ZIP _____

COUNTRY _____ COUNTY (NY residents only) _____

TEL _____ FAX _____

E-MAIL_____
May we use your e-mail address for confirmations and other types of information? ☐ Yes   ☐ No

Order From Your Local Bookstore or Directly From
The Haworth Press, Inc.
10 Alice Street, Binghamton, New York 13904-1580 • USA
TELEPHONE: 1-800-HAWORTH (1-800-429-6784) / Outside US/Canada: (607) 722-5857
FAX: 1-800-895-0582 / Outside US/Canada: (607) 772-6362
E-mail: getinfo@haworthpressinc.com
PLEASE PHOTOCOPY THIS FORM FOR YOUR PERSONAL USE.

BOF96